To: DAD
FROM: JASMINE
WITH LOVE

The Book of the Shar-Pei
TS-150

t.f.h.

Overleaf: Ch. Mo-Ti "Chops" of Beaux-Art, a Patrick Red Shar-Pei owned by Barbara Dion.

Title page: Shar-Pei owned by Gerald and Patricia Brown. Photograph by Isabelle Français.

Distributed in the UNITED STATES by T.F.H. Publications, Inc., One T.F.H. Plaza, Neptune City, NJ 07753; in CANADA to the Pet Trade by H & L Pet Supplies Inc., 27 Kingston Crescent, Kitchener, Ontario N2B 2T6; Rolf C. Hagen Ltd., 3225 Sartelon Street, Montreal 382 Quebec; in CANADA to the Book Trade by Macmillan of Canada (A Division of Canada Publishing Corporation), 164 Commander Boulevard, Agincourt, Ontario M1S 3C7; in ENGLAND by T.F.H. Publications, PO Box 15, Waterlooville PO7 6BQ; in AUSTRALIA AND THE SOUTH PACIFIC by T.F.H. (Australia) Pty. Ltd., Box 149, Brookvale 2100 N.S.W., Australia; in NEW ZEALAND by Ross Haines & Son, Ltd., 82 D Elizabeth Knox Place, Panmure, Auckland, New Zealand; in the PHILIPPINES by Bio-Research, 5 Lippay Street, San Lorenzo Village, Makati, Rizal; in SOUTH AFRICA by Multipet Pty. Ltd., P.O. Box 35347, Northway, 4065, South Africa. Published by T.F.H. Publications, Inc. Manufactured in the United States of America by T.F.H. Publications, Inc.

The Book of the
Shar-Pei
Joan McDonald Brearley

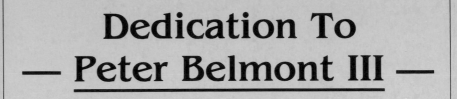

Dedication To
— Peter Belmont III —

My friend of many years' standing. It is through his suggestion, cooperation, and encouragement that this book became a reality. His contribution to the fancy, in many capacities, cannot be denied.

— Acknowledgments —

The author is grateful to many people for their aid in the compiling of this book. First and foremost, Peter Belmont, for reasons mentioned in the dedication and many others; to my veterinarian of many years' standing, Dr. Robert R. Shomer, V.M.D.; and to all of the owners, breeders, and exhibitors who so willingly submitted their photographs and memorabilia so that their wonderul Shar-Pei could be a part of this permanent record of the breed.
Joan Brearley
Sea Bright, New Jersey

— Contents —

About
— <u>the Author</u> —

Joan Brearley is the first to admit that animals in general—and dogs in particular—are a most important part of her life. Since childhood there has been a steady stream of dogs, cats, birds, fish, rabbits, snakes, alligators, etc., for her own personal menagerie. Over the years she has owned over thirty breeds of purebred dogs as well as countless mixtures, since the door was never closed to a needy or homeless animal.

Joan's early career was in the world of entertainment. She is a graduate of the American Academy of Dramatic Arts, and while an associate producer-director at a major network, worked on "Nick Carter, Master Detective," "Did Justice Triumph," news and special feature programs. She studied creative writing at Columbia University and has written for radio, television and magazines. She was a copywriter for one of the major New York City advertising agencies, working on accounts of Metro-Goldwyn-Mayer Motion Picture studios,

Joan McDonald Brearley, the author

Cosmopolitan magazine, the World-Telegram Sun newspaper, etc. Joan also wrote, cast, directed, produced, and on occasion, starred in television commercials. She has written special material for such personalities as Dick Van Dyke, Amy Vanderbilt, William B. Williams, Gene Rayburn, Bill Stern, and many other people prominent in the entertainment world. She has been a guest on several of the nation's most popular talk shows, including Mike Douglas, Joe Franklin, Cleveland Amory, David Susskind and The Today Show, to name just a few. Joan was selected for inclusion in the Directory of the Foremost Women in Communications in 1969 and the book *Two Thousand Women of Achievement* in 1971.

Her accomplishments in the dog fancy include breeding and exhibiting top show dogs, being a writer and columnist for various magazines, and author of over thirty books on dogs and cats. For five years she was Executive Vice President

Temple Toi Tepenyaki with his co-owner Lisa Berns. This brown horse coat male is eight months old.

of the Popular Dogs Publishing Company and editor of Popular Dogs magazine, the national prestige publication for the fancy at that time. Her editorials on the status and welfare of animals have been reproduced as educational pamphlets by dog clubs and organizations in many countries of the world. She has been an American Kennel Club judge since 1961.

Joan has been just as active in the cat fancy, and in almost as many capacities. The same year her Afghan Hound Champion Sahadi Shikari won the Ken-L-Ration Award

as Top Hound of the Year, one of her Siamese cats won the comparable honor in the cat fancy. She has owned and/or bred almost every breed of cat. Many of her cats and dogs are Best in Show winners and have appeared in magazine ads, television programs and commercials. For several years she was editor of the Cat Fanciers' Association Annual Yearbook, and her book *All About Himalayan Cats* was published in 1976.

In addition to breeding and showing dogs since 1955, Joan has been active as a member and on the Board of Directors of the Kennel Club of Northern New Jersey, the Afghan Hound Club of America, the Stewards Club of America, and the Dog Fanciers Club. She has received many awards for her work in the animal field, and is regarded as one of the most knowledgeable people in the animal world. Joan's Ch. Sahadi Shikari was the top-winning Afghan Hound in the history of the breed for several years, and remains near the top of the list ever since. No other breeder can claim to have bred a Westminster Group winner in their first homebred litter. Joan is also a former trustee of the Morris Animal Foundation.

This impressive list of activities doesn't include all of her accomplishments, since she has never been content to have just one interest at a time. She manages to dovetail several occupations and avocations to make for a fascinating career. She is a graduate auctioneer with full title of Colonel, a Daughter of the American Revolution, and a member of the New York Genealogical Society, a member of the Board of the National, State and County Realtors.

She also is a member of the American Arbitration Association, on the Boards of the Monmouth County Federation of Republican Women, the Youth Detention Center, and the Heritage Committee.

Joan's home faces the ocean in Sea Bright, New Jersey where she lives with her dogs, cats, and dozens of exotic birds. She is currently serving a second term as Councilwoman, is President of the Sea Bright Village Association, vice president of the Sea Bright Partnership, and an active member and Secretary of the Sea Bright First Aid Squad. In her "spare" time she exhibits her elaborate needlework for which she has also won prizes over the years. In 1987 she was appointed to both the Political Science and Criminal Justice Advisory Boards at Brookdale College.

Excellent headstudy of Ch. Boawncheins Argie Fu Chew, owned by the Boawnchein Kennels, Sunol, CA. The sire was Ch. Adam Fu Chew ex Chews Su Minga Ling.

"What Kind of a Dog — Is That?" —

Perhaps the question most asked of anyone who has a Shar-Pei is, "What kind of a dog is that?" We can only hope we all know how to pronounce it correctly, which phonetically is "Sha-pay". Kindly notice the "r" is silent. We can only imagine the various ways it has been said since its origin almost 2,000 years ago.

There has also been a great deal of speculation on whether or not the name is correctly used when and if hyphenated. Everyone I polled during the research for this book has not been sure, and admittedly I—and they—have always seen it written both ways on occasion.

As with all "points of order," we prefer to adhere to the American Kennel Club spelling and pronunciation of the name so it will be with hyphen included and pronounced sha-pay, until someone can prove otherwise.

WHAT THE NAME MEANS

In the Chinese language the word Shar-Pei means "sand skin." We know this to be descriptive of the coarse coat we breed for in our dogs. Indeed, it is one of their most fascinating characteristics. There are basically four qualities to look for in judging coat. It should be as short as possible, with no woolly undercoat, stiff or harsh to the touch, and sort of "stand-offish" or "sticking-out" from the skin. One of the greatest delights in the breed is the feel of the various areas of the skin, almost unlike any other breed we know!

General Description

The ideal Chinese Shar-Pei will weigh in at anywhere from 45 to 60 pounds, 18 to

Opposite: Ch. Temple Toi Tibet, bred and owned by Peter Belmont, of Kansas City, KS, exhibits the unusual padding on the muzzle of the Shar-Pei which has earned the breed the nickname of "hippopotamus" dogs. Tibet is a fawn horse coat.

Ch. Mo-Ti Chops of Beaux-Art, a patrick red brush coat pictured at six months of age. Owned by Barbara Dion, Sunrise, FL.

20 inches tall at the withers, with the coarse or "horse" coat about one-half inch long, with the brush coat approximately three-quarters of an inch long. Tongue and nose are black, brick or self-colored, the tail is tapered and the wrinkles are moderate.

So . . . the next time someone asks you what kind of a dog you have, you give the preceding general description and you explain that the name is Chinese Shar—(pronounced *sha*) Pei (pronounced *pay*). Then you can enumerate all their endearing charms.

WHAT ARE WE TRYING TO PROVE?

It is not the purpose of this book to name each and every Shar-Pei that has come upon the scene to date, nor to name every breeder, owner, importer or exhibitor who has helped to popularize the breed in this country. Neither is it the intention of this book to re-educate those who have been in the breed, or who have a general knowledge of all breeds of dogs and have had dogs all their lives.

It *is* the purpose of this book to reach those who are drawn to this unusual breed

as it exists today, and who wish to know the highlights of its history and background in the dog fancy today. The Shar-Pei has become so popular, so fast, that anything new that is said, shared or written about them can be of value to all of us if it adds to our knowledge regarding their care and place in our lives.

We would like to think that this book is dedicated to the mutual admiration society of those of us who love the breed, and that all who read it will accept it as the meaningful tribute to this remarkable breed that the author means it to be.

Ch. Glimmer Glen's Creme of the Crop, bred by Cathi Schneider and co-owned by her and Claire and Cowles Wilbert. Photo by Bruce K. Harkins.

Early
— History —

Let us assume that we go along with the modern-day scientific theory that the world began with what has been called "The Big Bang" approximately five *billion* years ago. This explosion of several chemical compounds and elemental substances, triggered by lightning and solar radiation, was a far cry from anything we might classify as living things.

In the billions of years that followed, both heterotrophic and autotrophic organisms began to develop and emerge from the oceans. They proceeded to survive and reproduce according to the theory of evolution, as espoused by Charles Darwin, according to natural selection.

Approximately 250 million years ago, dinosaurs and other strange-looking creatures roamed and dominated the earth for 100 million years or so. But it was as "recently" as sixty million years ago that a mammal existed which resembled a civet cat and is believed to be the common ancestor of dogs, cats, wolves, and coyotes. This animal was the long-extinct *Miacis* (pronounced Mi-ak-iss).

The *Miacis* were long-bodied, long-tailed, short-legged beasts that stalked and chased their prey, grasping it in their long, powerful, fanged jaws and gnashing their food with their teeth. Just 15,000,000 years ago, the *Tomarctus* evolved from the earlier *Miacis* and provided an even truer genetic basis for the more highly intelligent prototype of the domesticated dog.

It is only 15 to 20 thousand years since the first attempts were made to domesticate these

Opposite: Ch. Glimmer Glen's Wang Chung, bred by Cathi Schneider and owned by Claude Arsenault and Alan Griffen. The sire was Ch. Glimmer Glen's Chop Sooy Looy ex Ch. Doll's Handful of Magic. Photo by Bruce K. Harkins.

ferocious, tree-climbing animals. Archaeologists have uncovered the skeletal remains of dogs that date back to the age of the cavemen. Apparently, dogs co-existed with people as members of families in several ancient civilizations.

There are several schools of thought among scholars and scientists on the exact location of the very first creatures to live together with humans. Some contend that the continent of Africa was the original locale. Ancient remains unearthed near Lake Baikal date back to 9000 years B.C. In the 1950s in an excavation in Pelegawra, Iraq, a canine fossil (appropriately labeled the Pelegawra dog) was discovered and is said to date back 14,500 years. Siberian remains are said to go back 20,000 years. The Jaguar Cave Dogs of North America have been dated *circa* 8400 B.C. Others claim the Chinese Wolf to be the ancestor of the dog.

Advocates of the theory of the Chinese Wolf point out that a language barrier was responsible for the Chinese Wolf not being known or acknowledged in earlier comparisons. Because scientists could not translate Chinese writings, they could not study or authenticate the early Oriental findings. The theory is also based on the jawbone of both the Chinese Wolf and the dog. This major similarity is believed to be significant in the change from their being strictly carnivorous to creatures that eventually became omnivorous.

DOMESTICATION OF DOGS

The general consensus of opinion among scientists dealing in prehistoric and archaeological studies

Ch. Temple Toi Tibet, an excellent example of the short and harsh horse coat. He also exemplifies the proper topline in the breed—higher at the rear with tail set on extremely high. Bred and owned by Peter Belmont.

seems to settle on the likelihood that dogs were being domesticated in many parts of the world at approximately the same period in time. Since dogs were to become so essential to man's very existence, they naturally were absorbed into family life wherever and whenever their paths crossed.

Climate, geography, and other environmental conditions all played a part in the evolution of the dog, and much later, the individual types, sizes and breeds of dogs.

The three most primitive types originated in three parts of the globe. While all bore certain very exact characteristics, the wolf-type

Albright's Ten-E-Chu, bred by Ernest Albright and owned by Cathi Schneider.

(the Dingo) seemed to evolve in southern Asia, the pariahs in Asia Minor and Japan, and the Basenji in Africa.

The Dingo found its way north to Russia and Alaska, across what is now the Bering Strait, into North America. The pariahs moved far north and developed into the various northern breeds of the Arctic regions. The Basenji and greyhounds coursed the desert sands and hunted in the jungles of Africa when they weren't guarding royal palaces in Egypt. As dogs found their way across Europe, they served as guard dogs in the castles, rescue dogs in the Alps and mountain country, barge dogs on the canals, and hunting dogs in the forests. The smaller dogs were bred down even smaller and became companions and pets and lap dogs to the aristocracy. Kings and queens of the world have always maintained their own personal kennels for their favorite breeds and should be given credit for initiating and establishing certain breeds that remained over the years—many of which are recognizable today.

DEVELOPMENT OF THE BREEDS

While cavemen used dogs primarily as hunters to help provide meat (and to be served as meat as well) they also made use of the fur as clothing and sought warmth from the dogs' bodies while sleeping or during extremely cold temperatures. Dogs were to become even more functional as time went by, according to the dictates of climate or geographical regions. Definite physical changes were taking place;

these eventually would distinguish one dog from another even within the same area. Ears ranged in size from the little flaps that we see on terriers and Shar-Pei, to the large upright ears on the Ibizan Hounds. Noses either flattened greatly as they did with the Bulldog types so they could hold onto their prey and still breathe or they grew to amazing lengths which we see in the Borzoi. Tails grew to be long and plumey such as those we see on the Siberian Husky due to the need to warm the air they breathe in the Arctic by placing it over their noses. Legs grew long and thin for coursing breeds, such as the Greyhounds, or were bent and short for the digging breeds like the Dachshunds and Bassets. Skin remained "tightish" to supplement speed on the hunting or courser breeds while it became excessively loose and wrinkled on the Bloodhound and Shar-Pei to give an attacker a mouthful of skin before it penetrated a vital organ, or allowed the dog to scramble under obstacles without tearing skin. Sizes went from one extreme to the other,

Ch. Doll's Handful of Magic, bred by Doll Weil and owned by Cathi Schneider. The sire was Ch. Gold's Black Magic ex Ch. Chu'd Slipper of Albright. Photo by Bruce K. Harkins.

19

ranging from the tiniest Chihuahua all the way up to the tallest of all breeds, the Irish Wolfhound. Coat lengths became longer or shorter. The northern breeds developed thick, woolly coats, and dogs that worked in the warm climates grew smooth, short coats.

SENSORY PERCEPTION

As dogs changed in physical appearance, their instincts and sensory perception also developed. In some breeds, the German Shepherd for instance, the sense of smell is said to be twenty million times keener than in his human counterpart, allowing it to pick up and follow the scents of other animals miles in the distance. Dogs' eyes developed to such a degree of sharpness that they could spot moving prey on the horizon far across desert sands. Their hearing became so acute that they were able to pick up the sound of the smallest creatures rustling in the leaves across an open field or in a dense forest.

All things considered, it becomes easy to comprehend why man and dog became such successful partners in the fight for survival—and why their attraction and affection for each other is such a wondrous thing.

THE CHINESE FIGHTING DOGS

The fact that the Shar-Pei were originally known as the

Malinda Bulgin, daughter of Show Me Kennels owners Lawrence and Jackie Bulgin, and handler Jean Niedermeyer enjoy an afternoon in the park with two Show Me Shar-Pei show winners.

Chinese Fighting Dogs leaves little doubt that our Chinese Shar-Pei were part of that group of dogs referred to in their native land as fighting dogs, along with the Akita, the Mastiff, and all other breeds that were also used as guard dogs.

That they were specifically referred to as fighting dogs can be further understood when one considers the advantage of their coat. "Bristly" and rough enough to reject even the smallest opponents, and right up to the most formidable

adversaries, the massive folds of loose skin (like the Bloodhound's) allow the enemy the biggest possible bite. The enemy backs off with a mouthful of skin without ever penetrating the vital organs that sustain life. Dog fighting was popular sport in ancient China. The challenging of one well-protected Shar-Pei against another well-protected Shar-Pei could guarantee a prolonged battle for entertainment and wagering. A Shar-Pei in combat with another breed of fighting dog could usually

Wonderful head-on shot of Ch. Mo-Ti Chops of Beaux-Art, which gives an indication of where he got his name. Chops was a champion at nine months of age, finishing in two months with three five-point major wins.

predict a winner!

With this in mind, the Chinese found justification in breeding interchangeably with other fighting breeds to emphasize the fighting instinct and aggressiveness, rather than to perfect a mightier Shar-Pei, bred in accordance with a well-thought-out Standard. We regret what this meant to the Shar-Pei breed, but to

Down through the centuries of existence in its homeland, we must also assume that, like any other breed that might have out-lived its purpose or was bred to excess, it was used for food. Orientals have little reluctance when it comes to eating the meat of the dog, especially when there is starvation among the poor. We can only wonder if, as with the Chow Chow (whose very name has become synonomous with food), the black Shar-Pei were found to be even more palatable than the red-colored ones!

Today's dog fancy is privileged to know the ultimate delights and characteristics of the breed. The Shar-Pei is a wonderful companion and family dog; he is equally adaptable to indoors or outdoors, ideal in size, protective but not vicious, tractable, quick to learn, good with children when properly introduced, easy to care for, obedient, and unique! As curious as he is, he is always an attraction, always a crowd pleaser, and a great dog among dogs. Little wonder then that the Chinese Shar-Pei has grown in popularity to an amazing extent and lays upon all of us the responsibility of seeing that it is not corrupted, misrepresented or over-bred for the wrong reasons—he remains in his rightful place in the wonderful world of

Ch. Show Me Cameo, with his owner Peter Belmont, exhibits his pure white coloration with lavender-black mask and brick-colored nose, which is acceptable on this color.

Opposite: Ch. Show Me Temple Toi, a classic Oriental beauty. This deep chocolate color with black pigmentation is referred to and registered as a "brown" Shar-Pei.

just what extent this practice delayed the perception of the ideal Shar-Pei as we know it today can only be speculation. Happily, we see little desire to develop this breed to the status of fighting dog in today's culture, especially in the United States, where this onerous title seems to be given to the Pit Bull Terriers for leading contenders.

dogs.

You've come a long way, baby, since your first days estimated to go back as far as the Han Dynasty in 202 B.C.!

ORIGIN OF THE BREED

As with any of the ancient breeds, we cannot say for certain what or where or when was marked the date of their origin. As with all the previously mentioned fighting dogs in ancient China, we can assume that from the group emerged what has come to be the Shar-Pei as we know it

today. We can be reasonably sure that we are talking about a breed that is several centuries into its development.

We can also be reasonably certain that in the early days when man and animals were managing to co-exist on the earth, dogs of this type eventually were taken into families and began to serve not only as hunters with their masters, but also as guard dogs as families banded together.

As near as we can ascertain, the Shar-Pei is believed to have been recognized in the South of China, near the China Sea in an area known as the Kwangtung Province. It was in this southern part of the Orient that they seemed to have established themselves and it was here that they flourished throughout their history. Flourished until, that is, they were in jeopardy of becoming extinct with the coming to power of Mao Tse-Tung in the middle of the 20th century.

Never regarded as honest-to-goodness dog lovers, Mao Tse-Tung and his Communist regime took a dim view of the population of dogs in China. By the middle of the century, they were heavily taxed and were receiving exceptionally high attention as a food supply. Just as in England during World War II when food was at a premium, dogs were

Ch. Mo-Ti Chops of Beaux-Art with Lisa Berns. Owned by Barbara Dion, Beaux-Art Kennels, Sunrise, FL. Photo taken in February of 1987.

either consumed or were hidden by owners with a dedication to preserving the breed. Fortunately, many were successful and many survived the national slaughter. After the original depletion of stock during the 1940s when the Communists began creeping over the land, another slaughter followed during the early 1980s. Once again the breed was rescued from extinction by a man we must all pay homage to for his caring and foresight for the breed. His name is Matgo Law.

Matgo Law
 The breed was unknown in this country after World War II. As early as 1966, there had been a few imports, recalled only because of their unusual appearance, not because of another Oriental purge. But it wasn't until 1973 when Matgo Law and Chung Ching Ming desperately tried to save the breed. Matgo Law, through his article published in *Dogs* magazine, revealed the plight in his country. His Down Home Kennels in Hong Kong housed as many specimens of the breed as he could possibly handle, and it was his supreme desire to encourage their exportation to American breeders to insure a future.
 American breeders, always on the lookout for the welfare of our dogs, and

A group picture of Zella Llewellyn's winning Shar-Pei photographed at their home in Alvin, TX.

25

always interested in something new for the dog fancy, responded admirably. Mr. Law's replies to the article numbered in the hundreds and he knew his mission had been accomplished. The irony lies in the fact that there were not hundreds of dogs available to satisfy this new demand.

The Albrights

However, a dedicated dog man was among the first to respond and to import. Mr. and Mrs. Albright and their daughter Darlene Wright of California were enthusiastic then and still remain in the breed today, almost two decades later. Mr. and Mrs. Victor Seas of Walnut Lane Kennels were also among the first to be enamored of

the breed and import it. Other early importers were the Ted Linns, Ruth Fink of Ro Geans fame, and Lois Alexander, to name just a few.

REGISTRATIONS

Another matter for speculation is just how many would have been imported if a constant supply had been available, and if the American Kennel Club registry had not been closed to foreign—born dogs at that time, if they were not registered with the Chinese Shar-Pei Club of America, which had been quickly formed to protect the interests of the breed from the moment it was imported into this country.

THE BREED CLUB

The original club which took it upon itself to act as the governing body was first formed in 1974 in Vida, Oregon, where the first meeting was held. The aforementioned Mrs. Victor Seas was declared registrar and she issued the first pedigree certificate on November 9, 1976. The first Annual National Specialty show was held in 1978, in Hinckley, Illinois. Shortly thereafter, dissension formed in the ranks and the original club was split apart, resulting in the formation of a second club in the eastern part of the United States. By 1980, the disagreements had been smoothed out and once again the two clubs merged and have remained so since.

Such disagreements are understandable, although unfortunate, when a new breed is trying to become established in another country. Owners and breeders were scattered, and those familiar with the breed and its attributes were few and far between as well. It was often difficult to keep all puppies from a litter when good homes, especially show homes, were not easily found without the breed being recognized by the American Kennel Club, and a stud book nonexistent until 1980. Personal records were kept by those who saw the breed's potential, but efforts other than personal contacts were slow going at first.

By the middle of the 1980s, the parent club had registered over 11,000 Shar-Pei, and today it is still climbing. Needless to say, what Matgo Law and Chung Ching Ming feared the most—that the breed would become extinct—is no longer a matter of concern within the dog fancy. While there are virtually none remaining in China, they are now known and usually recognized for what they are, all over the world.

On guard . . . at Beaux-Art Kennels in Sunrise, FL.

THE CODE OF ETHICS

As with many clubs intent on preserving the correct Standard for the breed, the parent club developed a Code of Ethics, a sort of "I promise to abide by . . ." set of rules to keep the breed in check. A copy of this Code follows:

As a member of the Chinese Shar-Pei Club of America Inc., I agree to support and be governed by the Articles of Incorporation, By-Laws and Rules and Regulations of the Club; and by such rules, regulations, and policies as may be in force from time to time; I agree to conduct myself so as to bring no reproach or discredit to the Club, or impair the prestige of the membership therein; I agree to base all of my dealings on the highest plane of justice, fairness and morality; I agree to neither buy nor sell Chinese Shar-Pei dogs of which the ownership is questionable; I agree to conform to the accepted standards of dignified advertising; I agree when selling a Chinese Shar-Pei dog to fully disclose the characteristics of the dog, its physical condition and to specifically identify any known deficiency when compared to the Standard of the Chinese Shar-Pei in America; I agree to take immediate steps to correct any error I may make in any transaction; I agree to fill all contracts made by me, either orally or written; I agree to give aid to

Opposite: Ch. Albright's Mi-Pooh Bear. Bred by Doll Weil and owned by Cathi Schneider. Photo by Bruce K. Harkins.

Ch. ZL's Dallas Delight, one of Zella Llewellyn's dogs that has been shown in Europe. Dallas received a Group Third at the Nice, France, show, and BOS in San Remo, Italy, and Monte Carlo. Dallas received one of France's highest awards of excellence.

Multi-BISS Ch. Shir Du Bang, top producer, and Shir Du Farrah Ho at home with owners Lawrence and Jackie Bulgin. Photo by John Gillespie.

members in their quest for knowledge of the breed.

LOCAL SHAR-PEI CLUBS

After the founding of the parent club, it wasn't long before local, or area, clubs sprang up all over the country. These local clubs, like the parent club, have a board of directors, set their show and match dates to be confirmed by the parent club, elect officers, etc. To learn the name of the club nearest your home, you may write or telephone either the parent club or the American Kennel Club.

THE BARKER

"The Barker" is the name of the parent club newsletter. The editor of "The Barker" encourages contributions to this publication at any point in time.

BREED RECOGNITION

For anyone who is taken by a rare or unique breed—such as our Shar-Pei—the day of recognition and acceptance by the American Kennel Club is the ultimate dream.

So it is with all of those early breeders and owners and exhibitors who first took up the cause for the Shar-Pei. On May 4, 1988, we reached admittance to the Miscellaneous Class at the American Kennel Club-recognized dog shows. Let us hope this step in the right direction will lead to their eventual championship status in the regular classes. The uncanny popularity of our breed certainly indicates that this is warranted and we hope merely a question of time.

To keep up on the subject, one might contact the Chinese Shar-Pei Club of America, 9705 East 80th Street, Raytown, Missouri 64138. Should there be another contact for the parent club, a call to the American Kennel Club, 51 Madison Avenue, New York, New York 10011 will give you their latest contact.

Beautiful head-on shot of three-and-a-half-year-old Swinging C'mork. Owned by Beaux-Art.

SHAR-PEI IN CHINA

For many years Joseph Chan had Shar-Pei as he was growing up in Macau, China. He has gathered much material and information on the breed and has had some of his thoughts and beliefs published in dog magazines in this country. Mr. Chan believes that the Shar-Pei has almost become an endangered species in China, in spite of several breeders in Macau. He further tells us that during the 1950s and 60s the breed was non-existent in Hong Kong with all breeding and purchases happening in Macau.

I tried very hard to get in touch with Mr. Chan to get permission to include in this volume a reproduction of the Chinese Standard translated from the Cantonese in the form of a poem. The descriptions include such amusing terms as Grandma Face, Water Buffalo Neck, Iron Pellet Tongue, Mother-Frog Mouth, Garlic Feet, Dragon Legs, and Horse's Rear End. I somehow think *nothing* has been lost in the translation!

THE SHAR-PEI IN HONG KONG

By the mid-1970s when the Shar-Pei was really gathering steam in this country, there was cause for deep concern in Hong Kong. Once a focal point, "the yellow dog of China" members of the Hong Kong Kennel Club had ceased to take registrations and would not issue pedigrees because of the poor type. They were also barred from Kennel Club shows. Complaints

Paradise's Rag Doll, one-year-old horse-coated Shar-Pei owned by Jane Lemieux of Farmington, NM.

about those involved in breeding were so numerous at the time that the club found it necessary to halt any further acceptance or acknowledgment.

The club expressed concern over a specific kennel in the area that was "creating" a special Chinese fighting dog by combining Boxers, Bloodhounds and Bulldogs, and had exported several to the United States. The incorporation of the Sha-Pei (as they spell it) "looked ugly with too much wrinkles or folds on every part of the body . . . " They deemed the dogs far from the correct type of recognized Chinese Fighting Dogs.

SHAR-PEI IN JAPAN

Oddly enough, while the Shar-Pei enjoys an assured degree of popularity in China today, the Hong Kong Kennel Club has not yet recognized this "native" breed. The same holds true in the islands of Japan. One exception is the Cho Sun Shar-Pei Kennel of J. P. Chan, located in Hong Kong. Mr. Chan, who became fascinated with the breed as early as 1970, obtained foundation dogs from a Mr. L. Wing, and it is our hope that future exposure of Mr. Chan's breeding will inspire other dog fanciers to once again establish this breed in their native land, and that it will

world in Spain. He was considered the best example of the breed seen to date in Europe.

Mr. Mason is most anxious to breed but considered the dozen or so specimens in his region to be inferior and sees the need to go outside his area. In the meantime, he will be showing in Italy, Germany and France. During the early 1980s, the price for a Shar-Pei was anywhere from 12 to 18 thousand francs.

Top: Peter Belmont, of the House of Toi Kennels, with his foundation bitch Ch. Show Me Temple Toi. *Bottom:* Two champion Temple Toi Shar-Pei, Temptation in the rear and Trillionaire in front.

also spread to Japan.

SHAR-PEI IN SPAIN

Just as in most European countries, in the 1980s, Shar-Pei were reasonably scarce. We know of some sent there by the Shoestring Kennels in Texas, and one named "Chopsticks" did very well in Spain.

Owned by Ronald Eric Mason, Chopsticks, who lives in Barcelona with his eager master, by 1983 had won eight C.C.C.s, seven A.C.I.B.s, eight Bests of Breed, and one Excellent Certificate in the dog show

The Chinese Shar-Pei
— Standard —

As with any breed that has such a strong, established beginning in a foreign country and then has taken off on a meteoric rise in another country, as the Shar-Pei has done in the United States, it is only fitting and proper that we present in a book of this nature, both the Chinese and the American Standards for the breed.

Standards do not just "happen;" they are the result of much analysis of a breed that was predestined to serve a specific purpose. A Standard evolves as do the requirements necessary to achieve it. Standards, frequently referred to as "Standards of Perfection," aim to provide a guide to accomplish this. It supplies an example, a sort of comparison to use when evaluating your own dog or dogs, to better facilitate your breeding program

when trying to "breed out" existing faults and to enhance the desirable qualities you wish to pass on to succeeding generations.

Some people say that "everything suffers in the translation," or that things cannot survive being taken out of context. While this might be partially true, we do need a basis on which to build, and we must allow at least a little bit for improvement, or progress, in a world where "perfection" is the ultimate goal.

Over the years (actually, the centuries) breeds could not have helped but change slightly as a result of the balanced diet vs. table scraps, proper medical care vs. death of incurable disease and grooming vs. natural outdoor living. Obedience training has also served this purpose as it gives incentive when

Opposite: Ch. Glimmer Glen's Chop Sooy Looy, bred and owned by Cathi Schneider and Doll Weil, Glimmer Glen Farms, Sewickley Heights, PA. Photo by Bruce K. Harkins.

Left to right, Kipers Flame of Boawnchein; Kong, owned by Steve McClaine; Mini, owned by David Bardo; and Mai Wing, owned by Liz Montgomery.

outdoor purposes are not available because of an owner's living circumstances.

If we are to live with and enjoy our dogs today, we must make this adjustment from "natural" to "domestic" living for them as smooth and productive as possible.

It can be done! We are doing it!

So let us compare the Chinese Shar-Pei Standard as translated by Matgo Law and the associates of the Hong Kong-Kowloon Kennel Association with that devised by the Chinese Shar-Pei Club of America.

THE CHINESE SHAR-PEI STANDARD OF PERFECTION (Chinese Version)

(Translated by Matgo Law and associates of the Hong Kong-Kowloon Kennel Association)

General Appearance An active, compact, short-coupled dog, well knit in frame giving a square build, standing firm on ground with the calm and firm stature of a severe warrior.

Ears Small, rather thick, equilateral triangular in shape and slightly rounded at the tip, set well forward over the eyes and wide apart. Contrast to the Chow, the ears should set as tightly to the skull and small as possible. It minimizes the opportunity of his opponent to get a grip on his ears. Some specimens have ears so small as the size of a human thumb nail; just covering the ear burr.

Head and Skull Skull flat and broad, rather large in proportion with the body, with little stop. Profuse and fine wrinkles appear upon the forehead and cheek, and continue to form the heavy dewlaps. Muzzle moderately long and broad from the eyes to the point of nose (without any suggestion of tapering but rather in the mouth-shape of a hippopotamus).

Above: Beaux-Art Red Hot Lover goes Best Puppy in Show at a May 1987 show. Bred and owned by Beaux-Art Kennels. *Left:* BIS winner Ch. Temple Toi Treasure Royale, aka Rambo, was sired by Ch. Alamo Acres Taisho ex Ch. Show Me Temple Toi, was one of the top-winning dogs in the Midwest for 1987, and served as the foundation stud at Ann Coleman's Tail's End Kennels in Miami, OK.

Eyes Dark, small, almond shaped and sunken (a light color is found in cream and light fawn dogs). The sunken small eyes are advantageous to reduce chances of injury to the eyes. Also the sunken eyes and wrinkles upon the forehead help the scowling expression of the breed.

Nose Black, large and wide, occasionally there are cream dogs with light-colored nose and light fawn dogs with self-colored nose, but a black nose is preferable.

Mouth Teeth strong and level, giving scissor bite. The canines are somewhat curved (increasing the difficulty of freeing the grip).

Tongue bluish black. Flews and roof of mouth black. Gums preferably black.

Neck Strong, full, set well on the shoulders with heavy folding skin and abundant dewlap.

Forequarters Shoulders muscular and sloping. Forelegs straight with moderate length and good bones.

Body Chest broad and deep, back short; the lowest part of the backline is just behind the withers and rises to the loin. The backline is similar to that of a Bulldog yet not as sunken as the latter. Echoing the wrinkles and dewlap, a lot of skin folding on the body. The abundant

Ch. Glimmer Glen's Chop Sooy Looy gets his show career off to a good start at this 1985 show. Bred by Cathi Schneider and co-owned by her with Linda McCoy.

loose skin allows spaces for the warrior to turn and attack even though certain parts of the body are gripped by his opponent. **Tail** Thick and round at the base then evenly tapering to a fine point. The three ways of carriage are described as follows in order of merit. The most desirable is the type set on top and curled tightly over to either side. Some specimens curl so tightly as to present the shape of a small ringlet, only in the size of a large ancient China coin. The second type is curled in a loose ring. The third type is carried high in a curve towards the back, not touching the back. This carriage allows the dog to wiggle in a happier and more eager fashion. On either type, the tail should be set high up on the loin showing the anus. A curled tail is most preferred.

Hindquarters Hindquarters muscular and strong, hocks slightly bent and well let down; giving length and strength from loins to hock. (Not as straight as the Chow.)

Coat Another peculiar feature of the breed. The coat is extremely short (shorter than a Bulldog's and a similar coat is considered to be too long) and bristly; and unusually harsh to touch. A coat absolutely uncomfortable to be held in any canine mouth. It is not lustrous as the coat of a Doberman, but

Beaux-Art Kennels' Temple Toi Tepenyaki won Best Puppy and BOS Puppy awards at just three months of age.

by no means gives the impression of an unhealthy coat.

Color Whole colors—Black, red, deep fawn, light fawn and cream frequently shaded (the underpart of tail and back of thighs of a lighter color), but not in patches or parti-colored. This is what the standard says about colors. "The Shar-Pei should always be a solid color, never parti-colored. Shadings in the blacks and fawns are very common and not indicative of parti-colors. Parti-colors, brindles, and black and tans should definitely be penalized and certainly not used in breeding program." Matgo S.H. Law. March 1980.

Black: Often shaded; nose black, born black; quite easily turn to a rusted-grey color in long exposure to sunshine.

Fawn: Deeper or lighter shade of cinnamon (in American Chow's language); often shaded; nose black; is born flesh-color and turns black in about a week's time. Most common color.

Red: Also shaded, but not so distinctive as blacks or fawns; nose black; deep red color is not common.

Cream: Shaded; fawn ears and always associated with brick-colored nose with black rim (this is why this color is not termed 'white') but eye color should be deep brown and tongue color should be completely blue-black, as blue-black as the blacks and fawns.

Dilute: Theoretically, cream is a dilute color but the writer tried to distinguish the following described color variety from the 'creams' and termed it 'dilute.' The coat color is a deeper tone of reddish cream; the color of 'hot cream' in the language of Persian cat breeders. The nose color is lighter brick-colored (lighter than the creams) without dark pigment around the rim. Eye color is usually lighter and the main difference is the tongue color—a shade of overall light purple instead of solid blue-black. If the overall color pattern is not diluted to an excessive degree, this color is

Top: Lyn Bar's Yang of Boawnchien, black horse coat at seven months old. The sire was Ch. Gold's Black Magic ex Ch. Tai-Chi of Chew. Owned by Paul and Rachel Ginsberg. Breeder-judge, Peter Belmont. *Bottom:* Best Brood Bitch at the Arizona Specialty show was Ch. Doll's Handful of Magic. Judge Jane Lemieux presents the win. Also shown are two of Magic's get, Ch. Glimmer Glen's Wang Chung, with Heather Schneider, and Glimmer Glen's Whoopie II, with Cathi Schneider.

acceptable.

Rust: An overall rusty-gray (not a seasonal rusted-black color and much lighter overall color than the former); the intermixture of black and fawn hairs; shaded, darker along the top of the back, fawn-rusty on legs; the overall appearance of a whole-color effect is maintained and no suggestion of distinctive border between darker and lighter color regions. Nose black.

Chocolate: A whole chocolate color with a chocolate nose and yellowish eyes; tongue color is light purple; it is whole colored, therefore, acceptable. The writer has so far seen only one of this color, born from both black parents.

Except those specially mentioned, the tongue color of all these color varieties should be completely blue-black. The stronger and deeper pigments are favored.

Weight and Size Around 18 to 20 inches at withers; weight 40 to 50 pounds. Dog is heavier than bitch and more square built. The well-balance of an individual is important.

Feet Moderate in size, compact and firmly set, toes well split up, with high knuckles; giving a firm stand.

Faults Spotted tongue. Tail carried horizontally or covering the anus. A flat, long shining coat (the coat is not harsh and offstanding). Tapering muzzles like a fox (not blunt enough).

CHINESE SHAR-PEI CLUB OF AMERICA, INC.

Standard of the Chinese Shar-Pei in America
Revised 10/1/82

General Appearance An active, compact dog of medium size and substance, square in profile, close coupled, the head somewhat large for the body. The short harsh coat, the loose skin covering the head and the body and the typical muzzle shape imparts to the Shar-Pei a unique individual stamp peculiar to him alone. The loose skin and wrinkles are superabundant in puppies but these features are less exaggerated in the adult.

Head Large, proudly carried and covered with profuse and fine wrinkles on the forehead and cheek. *Skull*—Flat and broad, the stop moderately defined, the length from nose to stop is approximately the same as from stop to occiput. *Muzzle*—One of the distinctive features of the breed. It is broad and full with no suggestion of snipiness. The lips and top of muzzle are well padded causing a slight bulge at the base of the nose. When viewed from the front, the bottom jaw appears to be wider than the top jaw due to the excessive padding of the lips. *Nose*—Large and wide and darkly pigmented, preferably black, but any color nose conforming to the general coat color of the dog is acceptable. *Teeth*—Strong, meeting in a scissors bite, the canines somewhat curved. *Eyes*—Dark, extremely small, almond shaped and sunken displaying a scowling expression. A somewhat lighter eye color is acceptable in lighter colored dogs. *Ears*—Extremely small rather thick, equilateral triangles in shape, slightly rounded at the tips. They lie flat against the head and are

Temple Toi Tattoo, a typical, "teeming with type" Shar-Pei, displaying the ideal tiny curled, wrinkled ear; proper head size; and short, harsh, velour-type coat texture. Bred and owned by Peter Belmont.

set wide apart and forward on the skull with the tips pointing toward the eyes. The ears are not without erectile power but a prick ear is a major fault. *Tongue, Roof of Mouth, Gums and Flews*—Solid bluish black is preferred. Light purple or spotted (flowered) mouths are acceptable. A solid pink tongue is a major fault.

Body *Neck*—Medium length, strong, full and set well into the shoulders. There are heavy folds of loose skin and abundant dewlap about the neck and throat. *Back*—Short and close coupled, the topline dips slightly behind the withers slightly rising over the short, broad loin. *Chest*—Broad and deep with the brisket extending to the elbow and rising slightly under the loin. *Croup*—Slightly sloping with the base of the tail set extremely high, clearly exposing a protruding anus. *Tail*—Thick and round at the base, tapering to a fine point and curling over the back. Absence of a tail is a major fault.

Forequarters *Shoulders*—Muscular, well laid back and sloping. *Forelegs*—When viewed from the front, straight, moderately spaced with elbows close to the body. When viewed from the side, the forelegs are straight, the pasterns slightly bent, strong and flexible. The bone is substantial but never heavy and is of moderate length. *Feet*—Moderate in size, compact, well knuckled up

Judge Peter Belmont awards BIS to Ch. Alamo Acre Taisho, handled by owner JoAnn Kusumoto. Taisho was the first dilute cream Shar-Pei to gain a championship title in the U.S.A. This win was at the 1985 California Specialty.

Temple Toi Tasmin winning Best Puppy in Show at the 1987 Chinese Shar-Pei Fanciers of South Florida show with owner Lisa Berns.

and firmly set. *Dewclaws*— Removal of front dewclaws is optional.

Hindquarters Muscular, strong and moderately angulated, the hock well let down. *Dewclaws*—Hind dewclaws should be removed.

Coat The extremely harsh coat is one of the distinguishing features of the breed. The coat is absolutely straight and offstanding on the main trunk of the body but generally lies somewhat flatter on the limbs, there is no undercoat. The coat appears healthy without being shiny or lustrous. A coat over one inch is a major fault. The Shar-Pei is shown in as natural a state as is consistent with good grooming. The coat must not be trimmed in any way. A coat which has been trimmed is to be severely penalized.

Color Solid colors. A solid-colored dog may have shading but not in patches or spots. A dog which is patched or spotted is a major fault.

Gait Free and balanced with the rear feet tending to converge on a center line of gravity when the dog moves at a vigorous trot.

Size Average height is 18 to 20 inches at the withers. Average weight is 35 to 55 pounds. The dog is usually larger and more square bodied than the bitch but in either case should appear well proportioned.

Temperament Alert, dignified, lordly, scowling, discerning, sober and snobbish, essentially independent and somewhat standoffish but extreme in his devotion.

The Chinese Shar-Pei
— as a Breed —

TEMPERAMENT

It would be difficult, if not impossible, to pass by a Shar-Pei and not wonder about him, whether you are attending a dog show or merely walking on the street. Their unusualness makes it difficult for the untrained eye to determine just from their looks if they are friend or foe.

Almost since their early appearance in this country, there have been some outrageous stories about the breed's temperament. They do fall into the category of one of the Chinese fighting dogs, which already have the stigma of being unusually aggressive.

We will agree for the most part that the Chinese Shar-Pei is, and always has been, a guard dog and defensive when it comes to protecting his home and family. More than this depends on the care and training by the owner who either encourages the dog to be aggressive, or socializes the dog from the very beginning so that it can be an enjoyable member of the family and a social asset in the home and community.

Common sense dictates that if you are in doubt about your dog's reactions to strange children, guests or other dogs, you thoroughly observe and practice all possible precautions to see that preventive measures are taken to preclude any such behavior that might lead to danger. *Any* dog bite is painful; even small dogs bite without provocation—so don't let it happen. You as the owner are liable to be sued. The Shar-Pei will seldom start a fight, but sure can end one!

Generally speaking, the Shar-Pei has a very steady

Opposite: An excellent headstudy of Peter Belmont's Ch. Temple Toi Temptation, an excellent example of the dilute cream with a brush coat.

Children and dogs just seem to go together naturally. Roby May and Ch. Albright's Mi-Pooh Bear make friends.

temperament, adjusts well to indoor and outdoor life, travels well, and is a good eater.

While the breed can be said to take orders well and learn easily, some of the younger ones can be stubborn at times. Early training, therefore, is advisable. Basically, they love children and other animals, and have been known when in country surroundings to exhibit a desire to herd.

To put it simply, the Shar-Pei can be wonderful family dogs.

CHINESE SHAR-PEI COLORS

In a general sense, there are many variations on a theme, and so goes it with the color spectrum in the Shar-Pei. Solid colors such as black, red, light and dark fawn, and cream are most desirable, with patches or parti-color undesirable. Shadings are sometimes visible in blacks and fawns and frequently the underside of the tail and back of the thighs are a little lighter in color.

As mentioned elsewhere, there is a certain group of people trying to perpetuate and establish parti-colors, but this color, brindles and the black and tans are not to be encouraged. They are absolutely not to be shown and especially not bred or used to establish breeding programs with hopes toward eventual acceptance.

To clarify the colors a little more, we must note that the color black, as in most all breeds, can have varying degrees of shading. Even the blackest nose can fade slightly from prolonged exposure to the direct sun. Black coats can become downright rusty-colored under the same conditions.

Fawns have always been another color that can be hard to define. From deep to light to cinnamon, all are acceptable and usually shaded. While this is the most common color in our breed today, they must carry the black nose. Reds are also shaded, although uncommon to date. The creams are dilutes to some but are definitely the palest shade with lighter eye color, brick-colored nose and blue-black tongue color.

Rust and chocolate are two other colors we hear about. The rusts should be

solid in color, though shading may be detected with a mixture of black and fawn hairs. The chocolate will carry a chocolate nose with a yellowish eye color, and the tongue more of a purplish hue rather than blue. In all pigments, the deeper the color the better.

Fortunately, color in our breed is primarily a matter of personal preference. Let's hope it stays that way.

Top: Mrs. Ann Coleman of Miami, OK, at home with her three-month-old Afghan Hound, a Shih Tzu, and two of her Shar-Pei. In the foreground is Ch. Temple Toi Talala. *Bottom:* Zella Llewellyn's Cricket, Night Mis, Pistol, and Ping at the Shoestring Acres Kennels. Cricket and Ping are two of Zella's obedience-titled dogs.

FLOWERED SHAR-PEI

According to the Standards the Shar-Pei is and should be a solid-colored dog. However, as in many breeds, every once in awhile, especially since Shar-Pei do not breed true to color, there is a patterned dog which is referred to as a "flowered" puppy.

While these flowered specimens are not yet acceptable, there has been interest shown in giving them recognition (i.e., the Newfoundland fanciers and their Landseers, etc.), and that day may yet come to pass. There has been interest expressed in their acceptance in the California area and even a few have been seen at the match shows in that state.

It is up to the geneticists to speculate just how strongly ingrained this flower gene dwells in the pedigrees of today's dogs. Some believe the gene is potentially a problem for the future, while others feel that the variety of shades in the breed today are sufficient. Time will tell.

SKIN

One of the most unusual attractions of the breed is their marvelous loose, wrinkled skin, which other people never seem to stop marveling about when they see them "in the flesh".

While it is perhaps one of their most wonderful attributes, it does require at times some special care.

Just as some dogs, i.e., the Doberman Pinscher, might require some lubrication on elbows and hocks to prevent skin irritation, the Shar-Pei needs some attention paid to those deep folds of skin that are so inclined to gather dust, dirt or other irritating substances.

The folds of the mouth should be kept clean so that

Beaux-Art Chocolate Eclair and Chocolate Elite, the first two chocolates bred and whelped in South Florida. At eight weeks of age, they are owned by the Beaux-Art Kennels in Sunrise, FL.

bits of food or debris do not accumulate. A wet cotton ball, a cotton swab, or even a wet towel can take care of this after meals. The folds around the eyes should be watched carefully so that watery or runny eyes from wind, debris or any other kind of irritation can be removed. This is especially true of puppies who run around raising carpet dust or various seeds from grass or brush. This need not be a chore for you . . . just as you would wipe any dog's feet after coming in from the rain or snow before allowing it on the sofa or bed, just check out the eyes and mouth. Let it represent a "welcome home" to your dog and he'll appreciate the added attention!

You must also check periodically for what has been referred to as the "scourge of Shar-Pei," or demodectic mange. Shar-Pei are highly susceptible to this mite, referred to in technical circles as demodex canis. Excessive scratching is a clue to the onset of this problem, with dry patches on the skin that eventually, with continued and increased scratching, will become red and sore. The veterinarian can best prescribe the certain

Excellent headstudy of the breed. Photo by John Gillespie of a Shar-Pei from the Show Me Kennels.

medication for your particular dog so as not to over-treat with the unusual Shar-Pei coat.

SHAR-PEI EYES

Just as the Shar-Pei mouth might have a tendency to turn in, which can hamper their chewing, Shar-Pei eyes are also a possibility for problems.

Entropion is an all too common problem with the Shar-Pei and can begin as a puppy or occur later in life. There have been cases where puppies do not open their eyes, even at two weeks or more, as other puppies do because of the overlap of skin in the area. Sometimes just the top, or the bottom, or both eyelids are involved and require veterinary attention no matter at what age the condition occurs. In some of the more severe cases, it must be treated surgically.

By surgery, we mean a procedure referred to as "tacking". Small sections of skin are removed from the offending eyelids and stitched. In the more serious cases several tackings must be made. In addition to pain

and irritation, ulcers or even blindness may be the end result.

EYE TACKING

I certainly hope that neither old-timers nor newcomers to the breed fail to realize that eye tacking in the breed will not be tolerated by the American Kennel Club. Any surgical change in any dog of any breed is strictly forbidden. And rightly so. A dog should not be altered in any way to adhere to the Standard, or to make it cosmetically more appealing.

There are several breeds, such as the Chow Chow, which are prone to entropion, and should not be bred or shown.

As breed recognition looms on the horizon, let us not begin a pattern of breeding or showing Shar-Pei that are severely afflicted with entropion. It is difficult, if not impossible, to "breed out" of a line, so for the sake of the future of the breed, let us not get off on the wrong foot.

Procedures which require surgical removal of any eyelid tissue are not tolerated in any of the breeds recognized by the American Kennel Club.

SHAR-PEI TONGUES AND TEETH

Along with the Chow Chow, the Shar-Pei is another of the Oriental dogs that has a bluish black tongue. While the Chow Chow Standard requires it,

Top: Seven-week-old Shar-Pei puppy in the Oriental puppy yard at the Temple Toi Kennels in Kansas City, KS. *Bottom:* Cassie's Cant Mis-B-Havin, sable female residing at the Beaux-Art Kennels. Bred by Jane Mancill.

the current Standard for our breed merely states that it is indeed bluish black, and further states that the roof of the mouth and the flews are also black. It is hoped that the gums will be black. We do realize that tongues tend to get lighter in hot weather conditions.

One can only speculate on the reasons behind this color as a breed characteristic and if anyone really knows, I would appreciate hearing about it, true or otherwise.

While the scissor bite takes us across the world to the English Bull Terriers for the vise-like grip, why then are the Shar-Pei teeth described as "somewhat curved" in the Chinese Standard while the Bull Terriers are not? I would be interested in hearing any theories or research findings on this point as well.

SHAR-PEI TAILS

Those who inquire about the finer points in this breed are always charmed to learn that the old Chinese Standard states that the tightness of the tail should be such that it is able to "hold a coin." This calls to mind some of the frivolous Afghan Hound breeders who tape fifty cent pieces to their Afghan Hounds' tails to try to give them what nature did not . . . a doughnut ring at the end. This invariably drives the dogs crazy trying to get the transparent tape out of their fur—this practice is not to be encouraged.

Ch. Linns Ping, C.D., one of the obedience-performing Shar-Pei at the Shoestring Acres Kennels.

Top: Handler Jean Niedermeyer pilots Ch. Show Me's Royal Flush to another top win for owners Lawrence and Jackie Bulgin of Columbia, MO.
Bottom: Ch. ZL's Czar, European show dog with two CICAB C.C.s to his credit. Owned by Zella Llewellyn, Shoestring Acres Kennels.

THAT FABULOUS FACE

Among many of the endearing nicknames laid on our breed, a few are quite descriptive, especially when one tries to describe the typical head and expression. We've heard blockhead, bone mouth and meat mouth, to name just a few, but perhaps "incomparable" suits them best. No other breed has such an incredible "mush muzzle"—there, I've created one of my own—as does our

Opposite top: Headstudy of Shar-Pei owned by Peter Belmont. *Opposite bottom:* Headstudy of No. One top producer Ch. Shir Du Bang, owned by Lawrence and Jackie Bulgin of Show Me Kennels. *Left:* Shar Jacks No-Spa Boawnchein, owned by Boawnchein Kennels; sire was Ch. Boawncheins Argie Fu Chew ex Boawncheins Attila Te Hun.

fabulous Shar-Pei. With that distinctive rectangle topped by those little tiny ears, no one can ever call them snipey!

DEWCLAWS

Oddly enough, Shar-Pei occasionally grow double dewclaws. As in any breed, dewclaws on the front legs,

especially on show dogs, are usually removed for appearance's sake if nothing else. Dewclaws have a way of catching on to things and are best removed at a very early age. The same can be said for rear leg dewclaws, but for obvious reasons do not seem to cause as much of a problem as the front ones and are sometimes left on.

On a shorthaired breed when "neatness counts," they are best removed by a veterinarian. They seldom require a stitch, but their removal even within a short period after birth must be considered "surgery" and therefore, requires veterinary attention.

While some will tell you these dewclaws were used as a fighting aid in olden times, our dogs today do not need any such advantage, and in fact, dewclaws only cause problems in getting caught in fences, curtains, carpet loops, etc., not to mention that lack of attention to them will lead to a possibility of their growing back in a circle and penetrating their own legs.

This can lead to unnecessary infections, pain and suffering.

REGULAR NAILS AND EARS

Needless to say, all the nails on your dog require care. They should be kept as short as possible without cutting the quick, and since all dogs depend greatly on their feet and ears for protection against an enemy, the ears should be attended to as well. Cotton balls or swabs, used gently in the outer ear only will do it. Otherwise, see your vet.

Other than the aforementioned general good care, good food and occasional grooming with a bristle brush should keep your Shar-Pei presentable and loveable as a member of your family.

Ch. Glimmer Glen's Creme Of The Crop, bred by Cathi Schneider and co-owned by Cathi with Claire and Cowles Wilbert. Photo by Bruce K. Harkins.

Ch. Albright's Eric The Red, bred and owned by Doll Weil, Doll Acres Farm, Pittsburgh, PA.

SHAR-PEI PRICES

Right from their beginnings in the U.S., the purchase price of this breed has been high compared to the prices of most American-bred dogs. Five thousand was not unheard of or rare for those dog people who wanted to get in on the early establishment of this unusual breed. Even today, prices remain in the four digits for single sales or for breeding stock. In spite of the tremendous surge in popularity, this remains true.

Perhaps this is for the best, for it somewhat limits the number of buyers who can afford to get into the breed and the risk of exploiting its popularity. The fewer number of owners might aid in this endeavor to not over–populate the breed. However, there are those who claim that the price forbids many true dog fanciers from owning and breeding, which would help preserve the breed.

Dog prices can vary and fluctuate along with the popularity, but the main thing to remember in making a purchase in any breed is the old and true adage that you only get what you pay for. And surely they are worth having!

Comparative pricing would surely be the wisest move before buying the dog.

THE LOVE/HATE RELATIONSHIP

Perhaps no other breed produces such positive reaction upon first sight as does the Shar-Pei. Folks either love 'em or hate 'em, and their opinions seldom change from their first glimpse.

Top: Show Me Kin Lous Ching Lynn, dilute cream owned by Kim McCafferty of the Kim Lou Kennels.
Bottom: Ch. Glimmer Glen's Creme Of The Crop, bred by Cathi Schneider and co-owned by Cathi and Claire and Cowles Wilbert.

When one considers the huge flood of advertising that virtually took over the media once the breed came to the U.S., we must assume that there were more lovers than haters of our breed.

Name it, and sooner or later, there will be a replica or likeness of a Shar-Pei on everything from shirts and greeting cards to needlepoint and glassware, and whatever else you can think of. For those of us entranced with the breed, we are pleased and grateful, but can only hope that all the hype does not go the way of other breeds that have gained too much too fast in the popularity polls.

We must all see to it that breeding programs are kept under control while we and all dog lovers continue to enjoy the many lives our dogs have touched.

Santa certainly got what he wanted for Christmas! Six-month-old Ce-Te's Fiery Red Iyi, bred and owned by Connie Tarrier of Ce-Te's Kennels, Johnstown, OH.

Top: Dog shows can tire you out! Five-and-a-half-month-old puppy with breeder-owner Barbara Dion. *Bottom:* Ch. Show Me's Royal Flush making friends and giving the breed a good name.

also featured ZLs Dallas Delight on their December 1985 cover, and a dam and her puppies on the November 1987 issue. *Pets Supplies Marketing* got on the bandwagon at the same time with Shar-Pei cover dogs on the August 1985 and March 1987 issues. Equally pretty was Darlene Wright on the cover of the January/February 1987 issue of *The Barker,* the official publication of the parent club.

Not only do many Shar-Pei grace the covers of

Top: Champion and obedience-titled Shar-Pei owned by Z. Llewellyn. *Right:* Ch. Paradise Co-C's A-Lot Ce-Te, bred by E. and C. Gorman and owned by the Ce-Te Kennels.

COVER DOGS

The appeal that the breed has in the advertising field has produced many lucrative modeling jobs for dogs and their owners. Peter Belmont's Temple Toi Tangerine has appeared in many ads, has been featured in newspapers and magazines, as well as magazine covers.

Dog World magazine has

Top: Swinging C'mork and son Beaux-Art's Red Hot Lover. Owned by Beaux-Art Kennels, Sunrise, FL.

magazines, but many are behind feature articles concerning their illustrious history outside the dog fancy. Vivien Kelly is among those who made a first page feature on a local newspaper in Aberdeen, New Jersey. This kind of publicity can only introduce the breed to others who can read firsthand about all their endearing young charms.

Shar-Pei have also appeared in countless T.V. shows and one appeared in the Tim Conway movie, *The Billion Dollar Hobo.*

We were particularly delighted by a piece of art work featuring the Shar-Pei entitled "China Seas" in a DuPont full-page ad in an exclusive ladies' magazine promoting their textiles and wall coverings division.

Some Prominent
— American Kennels —

TEMPLE TOI

While enjoying a fabulous career in raising, breeding, and showing Afghan Hounds, Peter Belmont was introduced to the Chinese Shar-Pei quite suddenly and unexpectedly. He was asked to judge a Shar-Pei Specialty and while studying and researching the breed for this first important assignment, he fell in love with it!

After judging, Peter vowed to obtain the best puppy bitch in the country with the thought of breeding and showing Shar-Pei along with Afghan Hounds. This came about with his purchase of one of Ch. Shir Du Bang's top-quality daughters who received her first points under Peter that very day.

This beautiful daughter of Bang was the now legendary Ch. Show Me Temple Toi. Toi's first show was the Chicago Specialty where Peter showed her to Winner's Bitch for a five-point major from the Puppy Bitch Class. It was in honor of this unusual Russian-sable-colored bitch that Peter adopted a kennel prefix for his Shar-Pei, Temple Toi.

It was in 1966 that Peter's Afghan Hound kennel name of Elmo was established. It was this year that Peter saw his first Afghan Hound on a television show and has been a breeder-owner-handler of many Afghans since that time. A daughter of Ch. Sahadi Sinbad, bred and owned by author Joan Brearley, and litter brother to Ch. Sahadi Shikari who is one of the top-winning Afghan Hounds in the history of the breed, got Peter started. Through co-breeding with Sunny Shay of Grandeur fame and other established breeders, he was well on his way. Since then, his dogs have been

Opposite: A classic headstudy of Ch. Show Me Temple Toi, illustrating the flat skull, moderately defined stop, and small tight ear. Bred and owned by Peter Belmont.

among the top winners in the breed. His multi-Best in Show Ch. Elmos' Tutankhamun is perhaps his most famous along with Best in Show Ch. Elmo's Blue Graffiti, No. 2 Afghan Hound in the U.S. at one time, according to the Phillips System.

Since his entering the ranks of Shar-Pei fanciers, Peter has been affiliated with various magazines and educational journals, including *Popular Dogs* magazine, which the author edited for several years. He was also an editor of the CSP magazine, *The Elite*, and a contributing editor of *The Orient Express II*, and *The American Kennel*

Gazette. He has been a founding member of several breed clubs and has served as president or on the boards of many of them.

Peter had an impressive athletic career. He was a teenage figure skater and was an A.A.U. judge at just 16 years of age. He also has had an overwhelming academic career, compiling honors, grants and awards in the literary field. For over two years, he studied with world-famous anthropologist Dr. Margaret Mead. Anthropological phenomena is another of Peter's fascinations. After completing an M.A. degree at New York University and all course work for a doctorate at Columbia University, Peter moved to his current address in Kansas City, where Elmo and Temple Toi dogs share a five-acre "sanctum" for show dogs. It is here that Peter continues to breed, show and enjoy his dogs and judging assignments along with his numerous civic, charitable and philanthropic work in the State of Kansas.

BOAWNCHEIN

Bob and Dawn Walling of Sunol, California, purchased their first Shar-Pei in 1977. At that time they had two Afghan Hounds, and were active in lure coursing for a few years. That first Shar-Pei was a male named Eshafs Kan Tung which they

Bob and Dawn Walling's one-year-old cream brush coat, Ch. Boawncheins Sta Puf Lyn Bar. Boawnchein Kennels, Sunol, CA.

NOR. CAL. RARE BREED FANCIERS

RESERVE

WINNERS

DOG

FEB 8, 1987

Top: Ch. Boawncheins Argie Fu Chew at two years of age winning at a show. Owners, Bob and Dawn Walling.
Bottom: Boawncheins Comquat Shar Jak, winning her class at the 1987 Bay to Monterey Chinese Shar-Pei Club's show. Sire was Ch. Boawncheins Argie Fu Chew ex Boawncheins Attila Te Hun.

BAY
TO
MONTEREY
CHINESE SHAR PEI
CLUB

FIRST IN CLASS

APRIL 4, 1987
PHOTO BY JONNEE BARDO

purchased from Emil and Elverna Fahse of Cicero, Illinois. They were so entranced with the breed that within six months they bought a female, Boawncheins Ty-P-Bits of Eshaf.

Shortly thereafter, they began showing them at rare breed match shows, where five Shar-Pei were considered a large turnout. Within the next couple of years, more dogs were added to their kennel. They were Ho Wun II Mama's Bear from Darlene Wright and Lou Ells Ku Chi obtained from Eleanor LaTulippe. Soon after there was a move to two acres in Sunol, California, for their Boawnchein Kennels.

The Wallings have four children ranging in age from 12 to 25 years. While the whole family enjoys the dogs, the kids are mostly into sports while Bob enjoys judging and Dawn prefers to handle. They assure that they will always have a Shar-Pei, and really are not interested in going into another breed.

SHOW ME

In 1977 the Chinese Shar-Pei caught the eye of Lawrence and Jackie Bulgin after seeing a picture in *National Geographic World*. For the next two years, the Bulgins collected as much information as they could on

Multi-BISS winner Ch. Show Me's Royal Flush, with Malinda Bulgin, winner of Best Junior Handler award and daughter of Lawrence and Jackie Bulgin, owners of the Show Me Kennels in Columbia, MO.

the breed. In 1979 they purchased their first bitch, future Ch. Shir Du Farrah Ho, from Walter "Dugan" Skinner.

She became their foundation bitch, and they went back to Shir Du for a male with whom she could initiate their breeding program. The Bulgins later acquired multiple Specialty Best in Show winner Ch. Shir Du Bang, after seeing a picture of him at just five weeks of age. Bang arrived at Show Me in December 1979. He is their foundation stud dog and winner of many Stud Dog classes including the Shar-Pei Club of America shows.

As Bang matured, the Bulgins acquired the services of handler Jean Niedermeyer to guide his career in the show ring. His championship was won in just three five-point majors. The rest is history, as Bang continued his winning ways and distinguished himself as the top-producing stud dog in the breed to date, in number of puppies sired and sire of the most champions of record.

Some of the other top dogs at Show Me are Ch. Show Me's Royal Flush, Ch. Show Me's Impressive and Ch. Show Me's Temple Toi.

The Bulgins daughter, Malinda, also shows some of the Show Me dogs and is the winner of Best Junior Handler awards.

Malinda Bulgin winning at a Fun Match show with a Show Me puppy.

ALPHA

Another of the early advocates of the breed were Great Daners Pamela Hurley and Michael Litz. They saw the publicity for the breed in a dog magazine and started their Alpha line with a bitch from the California kennels of Ellen Debo. Her name was Hurleys Shen Te Mi, and quickly became their foundation brood bitch as her quality became apparent. She was to produce their Best in Show Ch. Alpha Chanel Moshu along with several other champions.

Their stud dog was acquired with Best in Show Ch. Shangri-Las Gogroila Teabaggy, a son of the famous Best in Show winner Ch. Shir Du Bang.

Pamela and Michael are particularly proud of the fact that Chanel earned the distinction of being the youngest Shar-Pei in the breed to finish her championship at just six months of age at a Specialty show. She was also Best of Opposite Sex that same day. At nine months of age, she won her first Best in Show over 20 competing champions, and makes three generations of Best in Show for their breeding line.

BRUCE LEE

In the early 1980s, Bruce Lee Shar-Peis became well known via their appearances on dog magazine covers and the ad pages of slick magazines. Bruce Lee, Resnick's kennels, located in Oldwick, New Jersey, are known for having produced many champions during their years in the breed. In fact, his "Dino," or Ch. Gold's Black T.N.T. has sired over 25 champions to date. Another top Bruce Lee Shar-Pei is Ch. Gik's Patrick of Bruce Lee. This exceptional rich copper-red has been used extensively at stud.

THUNDER MT. KENNELS

Jane Lemieux is the owner of the Thunder Mt. Kennels in Farmington, New Mexico where she also has St. Bernards and Flat-Coated Retrievers. But as she puts it, in the last few years she

has become "hopelessly involved" with this breed and as an American Kennel Club judge has been asked to officiate at many of the Shar-Pei shows where she has had the opportunity to see a wide selection in the breed.

She was the President of the Land of Enchantment Chinese Shar-Pei Club in New Mexico in 1987, offering her assistance in the attempt to get the breed fully recognized by the American Kennel Club.

BEN CHING

Formerly known as Kellys Kennels, Ben Ching, breeders of the Chinese Shar-Pei, got its name when Vivien's husband Charles won a world record title in

Show Me's Impressive, winning BOB at a 1986 show. Owners, Lawrence and Jackie Bulgin.

Right: Ch. Ivory Buddah's Shilah, at one and a half years of age in 1987. Owner, Jane Lemieux, Thunder Mt. Kennel, Farmington, NM.
Opposite top: A Ta Yang daughter, bred at Vivian and Charles Kelly's Ben Ching Kennels in Cliffwood, NJ.
Opposite bottom: Elly Paulus and some of the Honorable members of her Khan-Du Kennels in Somerset, NJ.

the bench press. Their kennel logo incorporates both ideas nicely and tells us that their kennel is located in Cliffwood, New Jersey.

While always active in conformation competition, finishing their dogs to championships, the Kellys have now moved on to obedience, lure coursing, and therapy. Vivien has given other dog clubs presentation on Shar-Pei and has done some judging for other Shar-Pei clubs.

Vivien was also on the steering committee which formed the Chinese Shar-Pei Club North East, and has acted as treasurer, show chairwoman and president for 1984 through 1987.

In November 1985, Vivien and her dogs were featured in a front-page article in a local newspaper where she received much good publicity and it also helped to educate the public to the breed.

KHAN-DU

Elly Paulus is involved in our breed as a breeder, fancier, judge, lecturer and author. Her husband Bill and one of her sons are both veterinarians and Rick Paulus is manager of their Khan-Du Kennels in Somerset, New Jersey.

Elly has been active in dogs for over a quarter of a century, primarily with Miniature Poodles and German Shepherds, as well as Bouvier des Flandres since 1985. Chinese Shar-Pei came along in 1980 and since then Elly has finished nine champions in three years as owner-handler. Her foundation sire has 71 Best of Breed wins and his

CHESAPEAKE KENNELS

Jill Parslow established her Chesapeake Kennels in BelAir, Maryland, in 1981. They moved to Delta, Pennyslvania, in 1985 and have been actively dedicated to the breed since.

There are three stud dogs at Chesapeake: Ch. Sui Yeen's Cai Hua, a fawn male; Ch. Chesapeake's Creme d'Caspar, a cream male; and Ch. Panache Outback Red Chesapeake, a red male.

Coming along are Ch. Chesapeake's Jelly Bean, a black bitch and littermate to Ch. Caspar, Ch. Chesapeake's Tobias of Me-Tu, a fawn male, and Chesapeake's He Lan, a black bitch that was Winners Bitch at the 1985 National Specialty in Ann Arbor, Michigan. She is a littermate to Ch. Caspar and Ch. Jellybean.

progeny are some of the exceptional dogs in the breed.

Elly is a member of several of the breed clubs including the Chinese Shar-Pei Club of America, where she has served as Eastern Director and on the committees for coat color and Standards committee consultant. She has also authored articles on health and genetics, and has been referred to as the "First Lady in Chinese Shar-Pei." This title is merited because of her willingness to always help others in the breed.

CE-TE

A 1979 newspaper picture of a Shar-Pei started Connie Tarrier on her way to her Ce-Te Kennel in Johnstown, Ohio. Her first Shar-Pei came into the family with Dobermans, which Connie was raising at the time in 1981. Her first was obtained from Mr. Ng Wah Chiu of Albuquerque. His Ce-Te's Mei Kim Fu Honwah became her foundation bitch. It was Kim that gave her her first champion, Ce—Te's Fiery Red Iyi and Ce-Te's Chocolate Hui Bing Low.

Connie is active in the parent club for the breed and attends the board of directors meetings. She also helped form the local Central Ohio Chinese Shar-Pei Club and has served as its president ever since— dedicated to educating newcomers to the breed.

KIM LOU

Kim McCafferty started her Kim Lou Kennels in April 1983. By September she had caught the "show bug;" she also exhibits Poms, Yorkies and Maltese, in addition to her Shar-Pei. She is quick to tell you that the Shar-Pei are her favorites!

In 1987 she had five Shar-Pei, two of which she kept from her second litter. All of them are family pets and live right in the house with the

Top and Middle: The Khan-Du Shar-Pei of Elly Paulus. *Bottom:* Ch. Panache Outback Red of Chesapeake, owned by Jill Parslow of Delta, PA. This red male was whelped in November 1986.

children and her husband, where the motto is "Kim Lou—where puppies are people too!"

Kim is the founder and club president of the Greater Ozarks Chinese Shar-Pei Club, the perfect outlet for her efforts to educate the public on the advantages of this marvelous breed.

Kim is also active in obedience circles in and around the Nixa, Missouri, area.

SOONER KENNELS

The Waldroops' Sooner Kennel in Coweta, Oklahoma, is based entirely

Top: Ce-Te's Toby of San Sha, bred by Connie Tarrier, Johnstown, OH.
Bottom: Ch. Paradise Co-C's A-Lot, at nine weeks of age. Bred by Ed and Carol Gorman and owned by Connie Tarrier, Ce-Te Kennels.

on their bitch, Ch. Eartha Doo Fang. Within Eartha's first three litters, she produced six champion offspring. All with the Sooner prefix, they are: Jassamine Tzo Tzo, C.D., owned by Jane Bryan; Geisha Doo and Abby Royalesun, owned by the Waldroops; Mizou Kasu, owned by Susan Stuth and Karen Kleinhans; Aw Gee Whiz Kasu, owned by Karen Kleinhans and Susan Stuth; and MarKe Golden Star, owned by Debbie Goddard and BJ Waldroop.

Eartha finished her championship at 18 months of age, and attended her first show in March of 1983 as Best Opposite Sex at just three months of age. She has been winning ever since.

The Waldroops' daughters Becky and Rachael have their own dogs and are active in Junior Showmanship as well as conformation competition. They train their dogs themselves and show them mainly in the Midwest.

TAIL'S END

Tail's End, owned by Ann Coleman of Miami, Oklahoma, was established in 1985. Tail's End got off to a great start with the top-

"Chigger," more officially known as Kim Lou's Ching Chigger Bang Boin, photographed in 1986. This exceptional red puppy was bred and owned by Kim McCafferty, Kim Lou Kennels, Nixa, MO.

RARE BREED
DOG
BEST
OF BREED   FINALIST

KENNEL REVIEW
MAGAZINE'S
TOURNAMENT
OF CHAMPIONS

Ch. Eartha Doo Fang, winning the breed at the Kennel Review Tournament of Champions in Detroit, 1987, was the first Shar-Pei selected as a Finalist in *Kennel Review Magazine*'s Tournament of Champions. Owned by B. and T. Waldroop, Sooner Kennels.

producing stud Ch. Shir-Du Bang as the sire of their very first litter. Branching out to the Alpha lines and then back to the Temple Toi and Bang lines, their breeding shows great promise for the future as well.

Tail's End is also the home of top-winning Afghan Hounds and Shih Tzu.

BEAUX-ART KENNELS

Barbara and Ronald Dion have their kennel in Sunrise, Florida, and are known to be very active in the breed. They established their

Beaux-Art Kennels in 1982, as both a show and breeding establishment and also housed champion Basset Hounds by 1985. Barbara discovered the breed while working as a veterinary assistant.

Their first Shar-Pei was Wee-Kare's Tai of Beaux-Art. He was also their first stud dog and produced many fine offspring. Tai also has the distinction of having sired the first two chocolate Shar-Pei in South Florida, their Beaux-Art's Chocolate Eclair and Chocolate Elite.

Top: One of the top-winning Shar-Pei in 1987, with several BIS wins, was Ann Coleman's Ch. Joss Commodity of Tail's End. "Commie" finished her championship at ten months at the 1987 National Specialty. *Bottom:* Ch. Temple Toi Talala, handled by Lori Wilson for owner Ann Coleman, Tail's End Kennels, Miami, OK. Sired by Temple Toi Tibet ex Ch. Show Me Temple Toi, Talala is here winning BOS over Specials under judge Rodger Prichard.

Beaux-Art's Peaches and Cream wins the Sweepstakes Two to Four Month class at the 1987 Dogwood City Specialty show. Owner-handled by Barbara Dion under judge Gary Sparschu, D.V.M.

Their efforts also brought about the founding of the Chinese Shar-Pei Fanciers of South Florida, with Ron serving as its first president.

Their first champion was Mo-Ti Chops of Beaux-Art. He was also the first male champion in South Florida, and completed his championship in the club on May 10, 1987, with three five point majors from the 6—nine month class and in just two months and one week of showing. All their dogs are trained and shown by Barbara.

They are also members of the Chinese Shar-Pei Club of Central Florida, the Atlanta Area club, the Southeastern Club and, of course, the Chinese Shar-Pei Club of America.

SHOESTRING ACRES
Dick and Zella Llewellyn have their Shoestring Acres Kennel in Alvin, Texas. For many years they owned Great Danes, but in 1987 they got their first Shar-Pei after their daughter Christine brought home a photo of a Shar-Pei puppy.

Their first "Linn" was purchased from Ted Linn's breeding and the second, Shouson, was purchased from William Morrison. These two females became the breeding stock for their kennel.

The Llewellyns are active in both the conformation and obedience classes, and their Linn's Ping was the first Shar-Pei to have titles in both classifications. Their ZL's Cinnamon Cricket has her U.C.D. through the United Kennel Club.

They have also exported dogs to Europe which have done very well, though it must be remembered that the Shar-Pei is not recognized as yet by the F.C.I. so they can not compete for world championships. However, they can be awarded C.I.C.A.B. certificates. Their "Archy" was a top-winning Shar-Pei in France and ZL's Frito Bandito of Texas won numerous CICABs and honors throughout Spain. Ch. ZL's Czar and Ch. ZL's Dallas Delight have won in Europe—Dallas received a Group III in a Nice, France show and Best Opposite in San Remo, Italy, as well as Monte Carlo.

Temple Toi Tepenyaki, a brown horse coat, owned by Beaux-Art.

Top: ZL's Obie Wan Kenobi, bred and owned by Zella and Dick Llewellyn. *Bottom:* ZL's Cinnamon Cricket, C.D., is the second dog to receive her U.C.D. title. Owned by the Llewellyns.

When the Llewellyns visited France recently Ch. ZL's Blue Genes and Dallas both received the high awards of Excellence in that country.

The Llewellyns favor the blue-gray color in the breed and are working on this in their breeding program. They also do therapy work with their dogs, visiting nursing homes to entertain, as well as local schools, where they educate on their breed and the general care and responsibility of dog ownership.

A nice selection of horse coat and brush coat puppies.

Showing and Judging
— the Shar-Pei —

Ever since I started judging dogs, I never enter a show ring to begin an assignment without thinking back to what the late, great judge Alva Rosenberg told me when we discussed my apprentice judging under his watchful eye. His most significant observation, I find, still holds true for me today—that a judge's first and most lasting impression of a dog's temperament and bearing will be made the moment it walks into the ring.

It has always been a source of amazement to me the way so many exhibitors ruin that important first impression of their dog before the judge. So many are guilty of dragging their dogs along behind them, squeezing through the ringside crowds, and snapping at people to move out of the way, just to arrive in the ring with a dog whose feet have been stepped on by people pushing to get closer to ringside and whose coat has been ruined by food and cigarette ashes. After all this, the dog is expected to turn on its charm once inside the ring, fascinate the crowds, captivate the judge, and bring home the silverware and ribbons! All this on a day that is invariably either too hot or too cold or too rainy. Not to mention are the hours of standing rigidly, while being sprayed in the face and all over the body with a grooming substance that doesn't smell or taste too good, and then brushed and trimmed until dry to their handler's satisfaction. Add to this the lengthy bath and grooming session the day before the show and the bumpy ride to the show grounds, and, well, Alva Rosenberg had a point! Any dog that can strut into the

Opposite: A Bruce K. Harkins headstudy portrait of Ch. Albright's Mi-Pooh Bear, bred by Doll Weil and owned by Glimmer Glen.

FIRST
PLACE

Glimmer Glen's Quincy, bred by Cathi Schneider and owned by Michelle Cervi. The sire was Ch. Glimmer Glen's Chop Sooy Looy ex Doll's Handful of Magic.

coming through." It works. Spectators promptly step aside, not only to oblige this simple request when politely stated, but also to observe the beauty of the show dog passing by. Those owners of small breeds who prefer to carry their dogs, and know how to do it without disturbing the dog's coat, can make the same request for the same result.

The short waiting period at ringside allows time for the dog to gain his footing and perspective, and it gives the exhibitor time to get his armband on securely so it won't drop down the arm and onto the dog's head during the first sprint around the ring. These few spare moments will also allow a great deal of the "nervousness" that travels down the lead to your dog to disappear, as the realization that you have arrived at your class on time occurs to you, and you and your dog can both relax.

ring after what could be regarded as a 48-hour torture treatment *does* have to have an excellent disposition and a regal bearing. How fortunate we are that so many of our dogs do have such marvelous temperaments in spite of our grooming rituals.

There is no reason why an exhibitor cannot allow sufficient time to get to ringside, with a few minutes to spare, in order to wait calmly somewhere near the entrance to the ring. They need only walk directly ahead of the dog, politely asking the people along the way to step aside with a simple statement to the effect that there is a "dog

ENTERING THE RING

When the ring steward calls out the numbers for your class, there is no need for you to try to be first in the ring. There is no prize for being first. If you are new at the game, you would do well to get behind a more experienced exhibitor or professional handler, where you can observe and perhaps learn something about ring behavior. The judge will be well aware of your presence in the ring when he makes a small dot or a small check mark in his judge's book as you enter. The judge must also mark all absentees before starting to evaluate the class, so you can be sure no one will be overlooked as he "counts noses."

Simply enter the ring as quickly and calmly as possible with your dog on a loose lead, and at the first opportunity, make sure you show your armband to the judge. Then take a position in the line-up already forming in the ring (usually at the opposite side from the judge's table). Set your dog up in the show pose so that once the judge has

checked in all the dogs in the class, he will have an immediate impression of the outline of your dog in show stance. This is also referred to as "stacking" your dog.

The judge will then go up and down the line of dogs in order to compare one outline with another while getting an idea of the symmetry and balance of each profile. This is the time when you should see that your dog maintains the show stance. Don't be nervously brushing your dog, constantly adjusting his feet, tilting his head, primping his tail, etc. All of this should have been done while the judge was walking down the line with his eyes on the other dogs in the

Ch. Glimmer Glen's Chit-E-Chit-E Bang Bang. Bred by Cathi Schneider. Owned and handled by Doll Weil. The sire was Ch. Shir Du Bang ex Ch. Doll's Handful of Magic. Bruce K. Harkins, photo.

Mo-Ti Chops of Beaux-Art shown with breeder-judge Gayle Gold at the Florida Fantasy Show. Chops was Best Puppy Dog in the Four to Six Month class, handled and owned by Barbara Dion.

class.

By the time the judge gets to your dog, it should be standing as still as a statue, with your hands off it if at all possible. Far too many exhibitors handle show dogs as if they were puppets with strings attached to all the moving parts. They are constantly pushing the dog in place, prodding it to the desired angle for the judge to see, and placing the head, tail, and feet according to their idea of perfection. More often than not their fingers are covering the dog's muzzle

or they are employing their thumbs to straighten out a topline or using a finger to tilt a tail to the proper angle. Repeatedly moving a dog's feet tends to make the judge believe the dog can't stand correctly by itself. If a dog is standing incorrectly the judge might assume that it just happened to be standing incorrectly at that moment, that the exhibitor couldn't imagine such a thing and therefore never noticed it.

Fussing over a dog only calls attention to the fact that the exhibitor either has

4 - 6 MONTH
DOG
SWEEPSTAKES
CHINESE SHAR-PEI CLUB
OF CENTRAL FLORIDA
SHOW B. HARKINS
1987

Circle H Sno-Cone Boawnchein. The sire was Ch. Lyn Bars Ying of Boawnchein ex Boawncheins Eppidermis.

to do a lot to make the dog look good or is a rank amateur and is nervously mishandling the dog. A free, natural stance, even when a little "off base," is still more appealing to the judge than a dog presented with all four feet barely touching the ground. All dogs are beautiful on their own, and unnecessary handling can only be regarded as a distraction—not as indulgence—on the part of the exhibitor. Do not get the mistaken idea that if the judge thinks you are working hard with your dog, you deserve to win.

Ch. Tail's End Rice Grinder shown finishing her championship under judge Olga Smid. This is a daughter of the legendary Bang, foundation bitch at Ann Coleman's kennels. Handler is Jeff Wilson. The sire was BISS Ch. Shir Du Bang ex Bruce Lee's Fan Nee.

MOVE THEM OUT

Once the judge has compared the outlines (or profiles) of each dog, he will ask the exhibitors to move the dogs around the ring so that he might observe them in action. This usually means two complete circles of the ring, depending on the size of the ring and the number of dogs competing in it. This is the time when the judge must determine whether the dog is moving properly or if it is limping or lame. The judge will check the dog for proper gait and observe if the dog is moving freely on its own—not strung up on the end of a lead with the handler holding the head high.

In the limited time and space you have to show the judge how your dog moves, be careful not to hamper your dog in any way. This means gaiting on a loose lead. Move next to your dog at a safe distance so that you do not step on him while going around corners or pull him off balance on turns. You must also keep in mind that you should not get too close to the dog ahead of you, and that you must keep far enough ahead of the dog behind you so that your dog doesn't get spooked, or so that you don't break the gait.

Once the judge has had time to observe each dog in motion, the signal will be given to one person to stop at a specific spot in the ring, forming the line-up for closer inspection of each dog individually. At the judge's discretion, the individual evaluation can be done either in place or for small breeds, on a table placed in the ring. Whether the judge chooses to evaluate each dog on the ground or on a table, he must go over each one completely in order to evaluate it in accordance with the Standard for its breed.

CLOSE EXAMINATION

As the judge approaches your dog, he will get his first close look at the expression. The judge will want to see the eye color and will want to check the stop, the muzzle, the occiput, the ear leather and set, and the head in its entirety for excellence. During this examination, the exhibitor must make sure the dog remains perfectly still and in correct show stance. Since the dangers of various viral infections and contagious diseases that can be passed

Bubba at five months of age. Black horse coat owned by Bonnie Patterson.

from dog to dog at the shows have been made known to us, hopefully the judge will ask that each exhibitor show his own. However, some judges themsevles prefer to open the dog's mouth, especially if they have reason to believe there is a fault. The judge will also evaluate the head from straight on, as well as in profile.

Next, the neck and shoulders will be checked. Shoulders play an important part in the proper placement of the front legs and pasterns. Running his hands down the front leg, the judge will go all the way to the foot, picking it up and checking the foot pads and nails and paying particular attention to whether the dog puts its foot down correctly in place when released.

The judge will check the brisket and the tuck-up, as well as the topline. At this point, with his hands going over the dog, the judge can determine the proper texture of the coat and the general weight of the dog. Judging the hindquarters should prove the dog's legs are sturdy, well placed, and strong enough to provide the strength for proper gait

Best Bitch and BOW at the 1986 Atlanta Fall Specialty was Nancy and Dick Deakin's Ch. Nankin's Mi-P.S. I Love You. Love was handled for owners by Cathi Schneider.

WINNERS
BITCH

PHOTO BY SIMPSON
9-7-86

Best Of
Opposite
Sweepstakes
DOGWOOD
CITY SPECIALTY
olden Photography

Mo-Ti Chops Beaux-Art winning over an entry of 97 in Spring 1987. Handled by Barbara Dion under judge Gary Sparschu, D.V.M.

and movement. This is also the time when the judge will check to see that on male dogs both testicles are present and descended.

Once the judge has gone over the dog completely, he will usually take a step or two away from the dog to give it a final over all view, keeping a complete picture of it in his mind to make the comparison with the dog he has judged just before and will judge after yours. This is the time you must still keep your dog "on his toes" so that when the judge glances ahead or behind, your dog is not sitting down, chasing butterflies, or lifting his leg on the number markers. Remember, training is done at home—*performance* is required in the show ring at all times.

Ch. Golds Rising Son. "Sonny" is owned by the Llewellyns.

INDIVIDUAL GAITING

Once the judge has gone over each dog individually, he will go to the end of the ring and ask each handler to gait his dog. It is important at this point to pay strict attention to the judge's instructions as to how this is to be done. Some judges require the "T" formation, others the half-triangle. Further observation of your dog may bring a request for you to repeat the pattern, especially if your dog did not show well during the first trip. It is important that you hear whether the judge wants you to repeat the entire exercise or merely to gait your dog "down and back" this time.

When each dog has been gaited, the judge will want a last look at all of them lined up together before making this final decisions. Usually the procedure will be to, once again, present the left side of your dog as the judge weaves in and out of the line to check once more the fronts or rears or other individual points of comparison. Some dogs may be asked to gait a third time or to gait side by side with one of the other dogs, should the judge want to "break a tie" as to which dog is the better mover. Because such deciding factors cannot be predicted or anticipated, it is necessary for the handler to always be ready to oblige once the request is given by the judge.

After the decisions are made, the judge will point to his four placements and those four will set their dogs up in front of the designated number markers on the side of the ring. Be ready at this point to show the numbers on your armband so that the judge can mark his judge's book. The judge then will present the winners with the appropriate color ribbons and any trophies won, and you may leave the ring.

Contrary to popular opinion, it is not necessary or even correct to thank the judge for the ribbon. It is to be assumed that the dog *deserved* the ribbon or the judge would not have awarded it. Handing you the ribbon is part of the procedure and does not warrant a thank you. The club, not the judge, is responsible for the donation of the trophies. It is not called for that the exhibitor speak to the judge, but if the win is significant enough so that you feel compelled to say *something*, a simple and not overly exuberant "I'm so pleased that you like

Tenth National Specialty show of the Shar-Pei Club of America in 1987 indicates the increase in popularity throughout the 1980s. Multi-BISS Ch. Shir Du Bang takes top honors. Owners, the Bulgins of Show Me.

my dog," or something similar, is still more than is necessary.

The thank you for the ribbon has, on occasion, become what some exhibitors like to think of as a "weapon." At ringside you can sometimes hear words to the effect that, "I didn't even thank him for that rotten red ribbon!" As if the judge had even noticed! However, it *is* expected that you take with you from the ring a ribbon of *any color.* To throw it on the ground or leave it behind in the ring so that the steward is obliged to call you back into the ring for the judge to hand it to you again is most unsportsman-like. You must play the game according to the rules. Your entry fee is to obtain the opinion of your dog by the judge. You must take the opinion of your dog by the judge. You must take the opinion and behave accordingly. If you do not like it, do not give them another entry, but you owe the judge the courtesy of respect for that title.

After this judging procedure is followed in the five classes for dogs, and Winners Dog and Reserve Winners Dog have been determined, the bitches are judged in this same manner. After Winners Bitch and Reserve Winners Bitch awards have been made, the Best of Breed judging follows. Once the judge has completed his assignment

ZL's Cinnamon Cricket, C.D., one of the outstanding obedience dogs in the breed. Owners, Zella and Dick Llewellyn.

BEST OF OPPOSITE SWEEPSTAKES
MID-ATLANTIC CHINESE SHAR-PEI CLUB
SHOW
1987 B. HARKINS

and signed his judge's book, it is permissible to request any photographs that you may wish to have taken of your wins. At this time it is also permissible to ask the judge his motives in his judging of *your* dog. If you wish to, it should be done in a polite and calm manner. It must be remembered that the judge is not going to make comparisons, rating one dog against another, but can, if he chooses, give a brief explanation as to how he evaluated your dog.

It is helpful to remember that "no one wins them all." You will win some and lose some no matter how good your dog is. Judges are human and, while no one is perfect, they have earned the title of "judge" for some mighty good reasons. Try to recall that this is a sport and it should be fun—tomorrow is another day.

Dave and Kathy Ruotolo's Glimmer Glen's Whoopie II. Bred and handled for the Ruotolos by Cathi Schneider. The sire was Ch. Glimmer Glen's Chop Sooy Looy ex Ch. Doll's Handful of Magic.

Boawncheins Comquat Shar Jak, brush coat red female winning at one year of age. The sire was Boawncheins Argie Fu Chew ex Shar Jak Tilly. Owned by Bob and Dawn Walling of Sunol, CA.

THE GAMES PEOPLE PLAY

If you are new to the game of dog-show exhibiting there are a few things you should know about, such as how to protect yourself and your dog so that you do not get too discouraged and disillusioned right at the start.

There may be an occasion where your dog is winning a great deal and jealousy will arise from others competing in the ring with you. It has been known that some of these bad sports will try to get between you and the judge so the judge cannot see your dog at his best.

Others may try stepping on your dog, breaking his gait so that he cannot be adequately judged, bringing bitches in season into the ring, throwing bait around to distract your dog, and so on. Needless to say, most judges are aware of these nasty tricks people play and will not tolerate them. Just be on your guard. Do not leave your dog alone or leave it in the care of others. Thefts have been known at dog shows, as have poisoning and physical abuse. Watch your dog at all times, and be safe rather than sorry.

BAY
TO
MONTEREY
CHINESE SHAR PEI
CLUB

FIRST IN CLASS

APRIL 4, 1987
PHOTO BY JONNEE BARDO

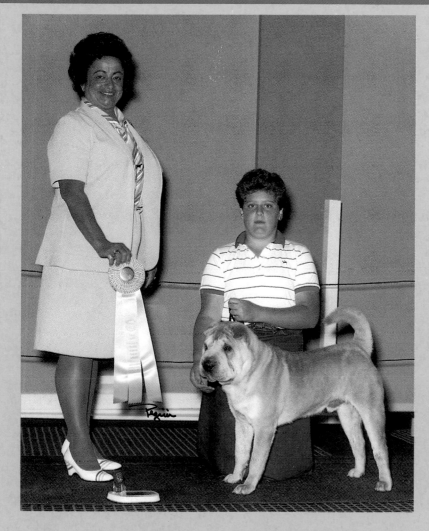

Heather Schneider wins Best Junior Handler honors at the 1983 National Specialty show in Houston, TX, with Ch. Albright's Mi-Pooh Bear, bred by Doll Weil.

CHILDREN IN THE SHOW RING

No one is more approving than I of children learning to love and to care for animals. It is beautiful to see a child and an animal sharing complete rapport and companionship or performing as a team in the show ring. Those of us who have been around dog shows for any length of time have been witness to some remarkable performances by children and their dogs. Junior Showmanship is one example; dogs caring for or standing guard over babies and infants is another example.

There is nothing "cute," however, about a child being allowed to handle a dog where both the welfare of the child and the general public are in danger. Dogs have been known to pull children to the ground with resulting injury to either child, dog, or both. I have seen frightened children let go of leashes or become tangled up in them in the

Ch. Temple Toi Tenno finished with three five-point major wins in 1986. Handled by Jim Deppen, Tenno was bred by Peter Belmont and is owned by Roy and JoAnn Kusumoto. Tenno's major wins were all at Specialty shows in Pittsburgh, Chicago and Portland.

middle of dog fights that left all three participants injured.

If a child shows the natural desire to exhibit a dog after having attended handling classes where he is taught how to properly show a dog, he must also be taught ring procedure. It is not fair to expect other exhibitors to show patience while a judge or the steward informs the child where to stand or waits for him to gait the dog several times before it is done in the formation requested. Lack of knowledge or repeated requests delay the judging look bad to the ringside crowds, and certainly don't make the dog look good.

If necessary, parents might stay after the dog-show judging and actually train the child in an empty ring. Parents should also sit ringside with the children to explain the judging procedures to them so they will know what to expect when they enter the ring. Many match show appearances should precede any appearance in a point show ring also. Certainly no parent could possibly expect a judge to give them a win just because they are a cute pair—even though they are!

BAITING

No matter how one feels about baiting a dog in the ring, we must acknowledge that almost everyone at one time or another has been guilty of it. Certain breeds are particularly responsive to it, while others show little or no interest with so much going on all around them.

There is no denying that baiting can be an aid to basic training, but in the show ring some judges consider it an indication that the training of the dog for the show ring is not yet complete. It becomes obvious to the judge that the dog still needs an incentive to accomplish what other dogs do in the name of performance and showmanship.

Frequently, tasty morsels of food are used to bait dogs in the show ring; however, squeaky toys will work as well. Using conversation and pet nicknames in trying to encourage the dog is inappropriate.

DOUBLE HANDLING

You may be sure that a competent judge becomes aware of any double handling, to which some of the more desperate exhibitors may resort.

Double handling is both distracting and frowned

Ch. Quehl Farm's Ace Tail's End at ten months of age. The sire was Ch. Trosanjon's Khan Quehl Farms ex Hei Te Fo's China Quehl. Owned by Ann Coleman, Tail's End.

GREATER MIDWEST
SHAR PEI CLUB

BEST BRACE

JUDGE M DOCKSTADER
MAY 21 1987
ST LOUIS MO
PHOTO J.G.

Best Brace at the 1987 Greater Midwest Shar-Pei Club Specialty show were Ch. Chu'd Slipper of Albright and Ch. Albright's Ugli Ermi, bred and owned by Doll Weil and handled by Cathi Schneider under judge M. Dockstader.

upon by the American Kennel Club, nonetheless, some owners go to all sorts of ridiculous lengths to get their apathetic dogs to perform in the ring. They hide behind trees or posts at ringside or may lurk behind the ringside crowd until the exact moment when the judge is looking at or gaiting their dog and then pop out in full view, perhaps emitting some familiar whistle or noise. They may even wave a hat or something similar in hopes that the dog will suddenly become alert and a bit animated.

Don't be guilty of double handling. The day may come when you finally have

a great show dog, but the reputation of an owner guilty of double handling lives on forever! You'll be accused of the same shady practices and your new show dog is apt to suffer for it.

APPLAUSE, APPLAUSE!

Another "put-on" by a less secure exhibitor is the practice of bringing his own cheering section to applaud vigorously every time the judge happens to cast an eye on his dog.

The judge is concentrating on what he is doing and will not pay attention to this, nor will he be influenced by the cliques set up by those trying to push their dogs to a win, supposedly by

Top: **Kim Lous Awsum Lucky Charm, whelped in 1986, is winning one of his three Best Puppy awards at one year of age. He is a harsh-coated Shar-Pei and is trained in obedience. Owned by Kim McCafferty, Kim Lou Kennels in Nixa, MO.** *Bottom:* **Ch. Doll's Pretty Prunella, bred by Doll Weil and owned by Mary and Joe Concialdi. Here Prunella is winning WB and WOB.**

BOS puppy over 98 entries from the Two to Four Month class. Owner-handled to this win in 1987 by Barbara Dion, Beaux-Art Peaches and Cream is winning under breeder-judge Susan Charles.

popular approval. The most justified occasions for applause are during a Parade of Champions, during the gaiting of an entire Specialty Best of Breed Class, or during the judging awards for Stud Dog, Brood Bitch, and Veterans Classes. At these thrilling moments the tribute of spontaneous applause—and the many tears—are understandable and well received, but to try to prompt a win or stir up interest in a particular dog during the normal course of class judging is amateurish.

If you have ever observed this practice, you will notice that the dogs being applauded are sometimes the poorest specimens, whose owners seem to subconsciously realize they cannot win under normal conditions.

SINS WHEN SHOWING DOGS

- Don't forget to exercise your dog before entering the ring. Do it before grooming if you are afraid the dog will get wet or dirty after his grooming session.
- Don't ever take a dog into the show ring that isn't groomed the very best you know how.
- Don't take a dog into the ring if there is any

indication that he sick or not *completely* recovered from a communicable disease.

- **Don't** drag the dog around the ring on a tight lead that destroys his proud carriage or disposition or chances of becoming a show dog in the future, if not that particular day.
- **Don't** talk to the judge while you're in the ring. Watch him closely and follow instructions carefully. Don't speak to those at ringside, and don't talk to your dog in an excessive or loud manner.
- **Don't** strike or in any way abuse your dog before, during, or after the judging. The time and place for

training and discipline is at home, not in public. Always use the reward system, not punishment, for the most successful method of training a dog.

- **Don't** be a bad loser. You can't win em all, so if you win today, be gracious; if you lose, be happy for the dog who won.
- **Don't** shove your dog in a crate or leave him on the bench alone until it's time to leave the show grounds. A drink of water or something to eat and a little companionship will go a long way toward making dog shows more enjoyable for him, so that he will show even better the next time.

Best in Match judge Rodger Prichard bestows upon Alpha Devil's Promenade the Best Puppy award at just three months of age. Jeff Wilson handled for owner Ann Coleman. The sire was Alpha The Headliner ex Moshu Bit O'Witch Tsal-I. This is a double-grandson of top producer Ch. Gogorilla.

Obedience
— Training —

Dogs shows and conformation classes had a big head start on obedience. It was in 1933 that the first obedience tests were held in Mount Kisco, New York. It was Mrs. Helene Whitehouse Walker who inaugurated these initial all-breed obedience tests that she had brought from England. Along with her kennel maid at that time, Blanche Saunders, they were responsible for the staging of the first four obedience tests held in the United States.

Obedience training and tests for dogs were an immediate success from the moment those first 150 spectators saw the dogs go through their paces.

Mrs. Walker was instrumental in getting the American Kennel Club to recognize and even sponsor the obedience trials at their dog shows, and her discussions with Charles T. Inglee (then the vice president of the AKC) ultimately led to their recognition. In 1935, she wrote the first booklet published on the subject called simply "Obedience Tests." These tests were eventually incorporated into the rules of the AKC obedience requirements in March 1936. It developed into a 22-page booklet that served as a manual for judges, handlers, and the show-giving clubs. The larger version was called "Regulations and Standards for Obedience Test Field Trials."

Mrs. Walker, Josef Weber (another well-known dog trainer), and Miss Saunders added certain refinements, basic procedures, and exercises, and these were published in the April 1936 issue of the *American Kennel Gazette*.

Opposite: An excellent headstudy of Kipers Flame of Boawnchein, red male horse coat pictured at two years of age.

On June 13 of that same year, the North Westchester Kennel Club held the first American Kennel Club licensed obedience test in conjunction with their all-breed dog show. At that very first show there were 12 entries for judge Mrs. Wheeler H. Page.

The exercises for Novice and Open classes remain virtually unchanged today—almost half a century later. Only Tracking Dog and Tracking Dog Excellent have been added in the intervening years.

By June 1939, the AKC realized obedience was here to stay and saw the need for an advisory committee. One was established and chaired by Donald Fordyce, with enthusiastic members from all parts of the country willing to serve on it. George Foley of Pennsylvania was on the board. He was one of the most important of all men in the fancy, being superintendent of most of the dog shows on the Eastern seaboard. Mrs. Radcliff Farley, also of Pennsylvania, was on the committee with Miss Aurelia Tremaine of Massachusetts, Mrs. Bryand Godsell of California, Mrs. W. L. McCannon of Massachusetts, Samuel Blick of Maryland, Frank Grant of Ohio, as well as Josef Weber and Mrs. Walker. Their contribution was to further

ZL's McTavish, bred and owned by Zella Llewellyn of the Shoestring Acres Kennels in Alvin, TX.

Barbara Dion of Sunrise, FL, with her Beaux-Art Chocolate Elite, a six-month-old male.

Standardize judging procedures and utility exercises.

A little of the emphasis on dog obedience was diverted with the outbreak of World War II, when talk switched to the topic of dogs serving in defense of their country. As soon as peace was declared, however, interest in obedience reached new heights. In 1946, the American Kennel Club called for another Obedience Advisory Committee, this time headed by John C.

Neff. This committee included Blanche Saunders, Clarence Pfaffenberger, Theodore Kapnek, L. Wilson Davis, Howard P. Calussen, Elliott Blackiston, Oscar Franzen, and Clyde Henderson.

Under their leadership, the obedience booklet grew to 43 pages. Rules and regulations were even more Standardized than ever before and there was the addition of the requirements for the Tracking Dog title.

In 1971, an obedience

Malinda Bulgin, voted Best Junior Handler, with one of the Show Me dogs. Photo by John Gillespie.

Falkner of Texas, Mary Lee Whiting of Minnesota, and Robert Self of Illinois, co-publisher of the important *Front and Finish* obedience newspaper.

While the Committee functions continuously, meetings of the board are tentatively held every other year, unless a specific function or obedience question comes up, in which case a special meeting is called.

During the 1975 session, the Committee held discussions on several old and new aspects of the obedience world. In addition to their own ever-increasing responsibilities to the fancy, they discussed seminars and educational symposiums, the licensing of Tracking clubs, a booklet with suggested guidelines for obedience judges, schutzhund training, and the aspects of a Utility Excellent Class degree.

Through the efforts of succeeding Advisory Committee members, the future of the sport has been insured, as well as the continuing emphasis on the working abilities for which dogs were originally bred. Obedience work also provides novices an opportunity to train and handle their dogs in an atmosphere that provides maximum pleasure and accomplishment at minimum expense—which is

department was established at the American Kennel Club offices to keep pace with the growth of the sport and for constant review and guidance for show-giving clubs. Judge Richard H. D'Ambrisi was the director until his untimely death in 1973, at which time his duties were assumed by James E. Dearinger along with his two special consultants, L. Wilson Davis for Tracking and Reverend Thomas O'Connor for Handicapped Handlers. The members of this 1973 committee were Thomas Knott of Maryland, Edward Anderson of Pennsylvania, Jack Ward of Virginia, Lucy Neeb of Louisiana, William Phillips of California, James

precisely what Mrs. Walker intended.

When the Advisory Committee met in December 1980 many of the familiar names were among those listed as attending and continuing to serve the obedience exhibitors. James E. Dearinger, James C. Falkner, Rev. Thomas V. O'Connor, Robert T. Self, John S. Ward, Howard E. Cross, Helen F. Phillips, Samuel W. Kodis, George S. Pugh, Thomas Knott, and Mrs. Esme Treen were present and accounted for.

As we look back on almost a half century of obedience trials, we can only surmise that the pioneers, Mrs. Helene Whitehouse Walker and Blanche Saunders, would be proud of the progress made in the obedience rings.

It was a sad day when we learned that Mrs. Walker died on March 11, 1986, at the age of 86. She will be missed—and remembered.

THE SHUMAN SYSTEM

Just as the Phillips System mushroomed out of the world of show dogs, it was almost inevitable that a system to measure the successes of obedience dogs would become a reality.

By 1974, Nancy Shuman and Lynn Frosch had established the "Shuman System" of recording the Top Ten All-breed obedience dogs in the country. They

Tail's End Kinni Kinnick at three months of age. This typy cream bitch was sired by Ch. Alamo Acres Taisho ex Fortune Cookie's Crystal. Owner, Ann Coleman, Miami, OK.

also listed the top four in every breed if each dog had accumulated a total of 50 points or more according to their requirements. Points were accrued in a descending scale based on their qualifying scores from 170 and up.

THE DELANEY SYSTEM

In 1975, *Front and Finish,* the dog trainer's news, published an obedience rating system compiled by Kent Delaney to evaluate

Tai-Li of Tai-Li, owned by Bill Morrison.

and score the various obedience dogs which had competed during the previous year. The system was devised primarily to measure the significance of a win made over a few dogs against those made over many dogs.

Points were given for both High in Trial or Class placements, as recorded and published in the *American Kennel Gazette* magazine. The dog that scores the highest in the trial receives a point for each dog in competition, and first place winner in each class receives a point for each dog in the class. The dog placing second receives a point for each dog in the class less one, the third place winner a point less two, the fourth place winner a point less three.

THE DOG OBEDIENCE CLASSICS

In March 1976 the Gaines' Dog Research Center, located in White Plains, New York, began its sponsorship of the United States Dog Obedience Classic. Founded by the Illini Obedience Association in 1975, the first classic was held in Chicago.

Gaines' motive in the support of the regional events and the Classic was to emphasize to dog owners, both present and future, their belief that an obedience trained dog is a better citizen and an asset to any community. Their support was to offer rosettes, trophies, and plaques, as well as prize money for a series of regional competitions and for the Classic at the year's end. Prize money for the regional awards was almost $3000, while the Classic prize money was in excess of $5000. Each year the Classic is held in a different region where a local obedience club plays host to participants from all over the country.

By 1978, when the two-day Classic was held in Los Angeles at their Sports Arena, people from 23 states exhibited with an entry well over the 180-dog limit, with dogs going through their paces in eight rings. The top winner earns the title of Super Dog and, along with other prizes and money, takes home the sterling silver dumbbell trophy.

The Gaines' Dog Obedience Classic competition is open to all breeds and owners who qualify and enjoy the challenge of team work with their dogs.

In 1980, Gaines began yet another award of recognition in the dog fancy. They began awarding a yearly "Fido" statue for outstanding achievement in the dog obedience field. Gaines' Steve Willett, Director of their Professional Services, made the award for outstanding contributions to the advancement of obedience training and competition.

OTHER OBEDIENCE ACTIVITIES

For those interested in the obedience sport there are many other activities connected with dog training.

There are Scent dog seminars, hurdle races, World Series of Dog Obedience in Canada, the Association of Obedience Clubs and Judges, to name

Daisy Garcia's Boawncheins Pearl. The sire was Ch. Lyn Bars Ying of Boawncheins ex Harts Toady Hart.

just a few. The best possible way to keep informed on activities on both a national and local scale is by membership in kennel or obedience clubs, and by reading dog magazines and newspapers published by obedience enthusiasts.

Front and Finish is perhaps the leading publication of the Delaney System and current subscription rates can be had by writing to H. and S. Publications, Inc., 113 S. Arthur Avenue, Galesburg, IL 61401. A. J. Harler and Robert T. Self are co-editors of this most worthy and informative publication.

The American Kennel Club publishes the obedience regulations booklet and offers it free of charge when single copies are requested. A check or money order for 15 cents per copy is required when ordering in quantities for clubs or organizations.

For those just getting into obedience work with their dogs, it is suggested that they obtain and read a booklet entitled "How to Understand and Enjoy an Obedience Trial," available free of charge from the Ralston Purina Company, Checkerboard Square, St. Louis, MO 63188.

Bred by Connie Tarrier, this six-month-old puppy is Ce-Te Chocolate Hui Bing Low. Connie's Ce-Te Kennels are in Johnstown, OH.

TRAINING YOUR DOG

While the American Kennel Club will gladly send along the booklets with the rules and regulations for competition at the shows, you must be prepared to start "basic training" with your dog long before you start thinking about entering obedience trials. There are few things in the world a dog would rather do than please his master; therefore, obedience training—even the learning of his name—will be a pleasure for your dog. If taught correctly it will certainly make him a much nicer animal to live with the rest of his life.

Some breeders believe in starting the training as early as two weeks of age.

Repeating the puppy's name and encouraging the puppy to come when called is a good start, if you don't expect too much too soon. Some recommend placing a narrow ribbon around the puppy's neck to get him used to the feel of what will later be a leash. The puppy can play with it and learn the pressure of the pull on his neck before he is actually expected to respond to it.

If you intend to show your puppy, there are other formalities you can observe as early as four weeks of age that will also minimize the start of training. One of the most important points is setting him up on a table in show stance. Make it short and sweet; make it a sort of

Ch. Mo-Ti Chops of Beaux-Art at five months of age. This patrick red brush coat is owned by Ron and Barbara Dion of Sunrise, FL.

Glimmer Glen's Obsession of Eric in his front yard at ten weeks of age. Owner, Cathi Schneider.

game, but repeatedly place the puppy in a show stance and hold him that way gently, giving him lavish praise. After a couple of weeks of doing this a few times each day, you will find the puppy takes to the idea of the "stand" and "stay" commands very readily.

Official training should not start until the puppy is about six months of age. Most obedience trainers will not take them in their classes much before this age. However, as the puppy grows along the way, you should certainly get him used to his name, to coming when he is called, and to the meaning of words like "no" and "come" and other basic commands. Repetition and patience are the keys to success since most dogs are not ready for a wide range of words in their rather limited attention span. If your dog is to be a show dog, it would

be wise not to forget to concentrate on the "stand" and "stay" commands.

The only acceptable kind of training is the kindness and reward method, which will build a strong bond between dog and master. Try to establish respect and attention, not fear of punishment. Give each command, preceded by the dog's name, and make it "stick." Do not move on to another command or lesson until the first one is mastered. Train where there are no distractions at first and never when the dog is tired, right after eating, or for too long a period of time. When his interest wanes, quit until another session later in the day. Have two or three sessions a day with a bright dog, increasing the time from, say, five to fifteen minutes. Each dog is different, and you must set your own schedule according to your own dog's ability.

The soft nylon show leads available at all pet stores are best for early training. Later, perhaps, a choke chain can be used. Let the puppy play with the lead or even carry it around when you first put it on. Too much pressure at the end of it is liable to get him off to a bad start. The collar shouldn't seem like a harness.

The Yellow Pages of your phone book can lead you to dog training schools or classes for official training along with other dogs. Usually they are moderately priced, and you might best start making inquiries when the puppy is about four months of age so you can be ready for the start of the training classes. If you intend to show your dog, training will make him easier to live with and will do credit to the breed, as well as to both of you.

OBEDIENCE DEGREES
There are several obedience titles recognized by the American Kennel Club that dogs may earn through a process of completed exercises. The Companion Dog, or CD degree, is divided into three classes: Novice, Open, and Utility, with a total score of 200 points. After the dog has qualified with a score of 170 points or better, he has earned the right to have the letters "CD" included after his name and is eligible to compete in Open Class competition to earn a

Ch. Glimmer Glen's Wang Chung, bred by Cathi Schneider and owned by Claude Arsenault and Alan Griffen. The sire was Ch. Glimmer Glen's Chop Sooy Looy ex Ch. Doll's Handful of Magic. Photography by Bruce K. Harkins.

Companion Dog Excellent degree, or "CDX", after his name. After qualifying in three shows for this title, he may compete for the Utility Dog title, or "UD," initials after his name. There are also Tracking Dog and Tracking Dog Excellent titles that may be earned, the requirements for which may be obtained from the AKC.

The Board of Directors of the American Kennel Club approved Obedience Trial Championship titles in July 1977. Points for these championship titles are recorded only for those dogs that have earned the UD title. Any dog that has been awarded the title of Obedience Trial Champion may continue to compete. Dogs that complete requirements receive an Obedience Trial Championship Certificate from the American Kennel Club and are permitted the use of the letters OT Ch preceding their name.

CHECK POINTS FOR OBEDIENCE COMPETITORS

- Do your training and have your lessons down pat before entering the show ring
- Make sure you and your dog are ready before entering a show
- Don't expect more than your dog is ready to give.

Heading home, Barbara Dion's puppy knows where he lives even at this young age.

Ch. Lyn Bar Ying of Boawncheins, litter brother to Lyn Bars Yang, winning on the way to championship. Owned by Bob and Dawn Walling. The sire was Ch. Gold's Black Magic ex Ch. Tai Chi of Chew.

Obedience work is progressive, not all learned in the first few lessons

• It's okay to be nervous, but try not to let your dog know it by overhandling or fidgeting

• Do not punish your dog in or out of the ring. If the dog doesn't work well, it is probably your fault, not his

• Pay attention to the judge and follow instructions exactly

• Pay attention to your own dog and don't talk to others

• Don't forget to exercise your dog before entering the ring

• Be a good loser. If you don't win today, you can try again another day.

• Have confidence in your dog's intelligence. His greatest desire in life is to please you if you have earned his respect and admiration

• If it isn't fun for you and your dog, stay out of the ring and try another sport.

Buying
— Your Puppy —

In searching for that special puppy, there are several paths that will lead you to a litter from which you can find the puppy of your choice. If you are uncertain as to where to find a reputable breeder, write to the parent club and ask for the names and addresses of members who have puppies for sale. The addresses of various breed clubs can be obtained by writing directly to the American Kennel Club, Inc., 51 Madison Avenue, New York, NY 10010. They keep an up-to-date, accurate list of breeders from whom you can seek information on obtaining a good, healthy puppy. The classified ad listings in dog publications and the major newspapers may also lead you to that certain pup. The various dog magazines generally carry a monthly breed column which features information and news on the breed that may aid in your selection.

It is advisable that you become thoroughly acquainted with the breed prior to purchasing your puppy. Plan to attend a dog show or two in your area, at which you can view purebred dogs of just about every breed at their best in the show ring. Even if you are not interested in purchasing a show-quality dog, you should be familiar with what the better specimens look like so that you will at least purchase a decent representative of the breed for the money. You can learn a lot from observing show dogs in action in the ring, or in some other public place, where their personalities can be clearly shown. The dog show catalog is also a useful tool to put you in contact with the local kennels and breeders. Each dog that is entered in the show is listed

Opposite: Ben Chings Shane of Viv.

Puppies bred
at the
Glimmer
Glen Kennels
in Sewickley
Heights, PA.

along with the owner's name and address. If you spot a dog that you think is a particularly fine and pleasing specimen, contact the owners and arrange to visit their kennel to see the types of dogs they are breeding and winning with at the shows. Exhibitors at the dog shows are usually more than delighted to talk to people interested in their dogs and the specific characteristics of their breed.

Once you've decided that this is the breed for you, read some background material so that you become thoroughly familiar with it. When you feel certain that this puppy will fit in with your family's way of life, it is

time to start writing letters and making phone calls and appointments to see those dogs that may interest you.

Some words of caution: don't choose a kennel simply because it is near your home, and don't buy the first cute puppy that romps around your legs or licks the end of your nose. All puppies are cute, and naturally some will appeal to you more than others. But don't let preferences sway your thinking. If you are buying your puppy to be strictly a family pet, preferences can be permissible. If you are looking for a top-quality puppy for the show ring, however, you must evaluate clearly, choose wisely, and make the best possible choice. Whichever one you choose, you will quickly learn to love your puppy. A careful selection, rather than a "love at first sight" choice will save you from disappointment later on.

To get the broadest idea of what puppies are for sale and what the going market prices are, visit as many kennels as possible in your area and write to others farther away. With today's safe and rapid air flights on the major airlines, it is possible to purchase dogs from far-off places at nominal costs. While it is safest and wisest to first see the dog you are buying, there are enough reputable breeders and kennels to be found for you to take this step with a minimum of risk. In the long run, it can be well worth your while to obtain the exact dog or bloodline you desire.

It is customary for the purchaser to pay the shipping charges, and the airlines are most willing to supply flight information and prices upon request. Rental on the shipping crate, if the owner does not provide one for the dog, is nominal. While unfortunate

A bevy of beauties, a typical bunch of Temple Toi Kennels treasures, bred by Peter Belmont of Kansas City, KS.

125

incidents have occurred on the airlines in the transporting of animals by air, the major airlines are making improvements in safety measures and have reached the point of reasonable safety and cost. Barring unforeseen circumstances, the safe arrival of a dog you might buy can pretty much be assured if both seller and purchaser adhere to and follow up on even the most minute details from both ends.

WHAT TO LOOK FOR IN YOUR DOG

Anyone who has owned a puppy will agree that the most fascinating aspect of raising him is to witness the complete and extraordinary metamorphosis that occurs during his first year of maturing. Your puppy will undergo a marked change in appearance, and during this period you must also be aware of the puppy's personality, for there are certain qualities visible at this time that will generally make for a good adult dog. Of course no one can guarantee nature, and the best puppy does not always grow up to be a great dog; however, even the novice breeder can learn to look for certain specifics that will help him choose a promising puppy.

Should you decide to purchase a six-to-eight-week-old puppy, you are in store for all the cute antics that little pup can dream up for you! At this age, the puppy should be well on its way to being weaned, wormed, and ready to go out into the world with its responsible new owner. It is better not to buy a puppy that is less than six weeks old; it simply is not ready to leave its mother or the security of the other puppies. By eight to twelve weeks of age, you will be able to notice much about the behavior and

A typical typy Glimmer Glen Shar-Pei puppy, and a future champion.

Five-week-old
Fantasia
owned by
Barbara Dion.

appearance of the dog. Puppies, as they are recalled in our fondest childhood memories, are amazingly active and bouncy—and well they should be! The normal puppy should be alert, curious, and interested, especially when a stranger is present. However, if the puppy acts a little reserved or distant, don't necessarily construe these acts to be signs of fear or shyness. It might merely indicate that he hasn't quite made up his mind whether he likes you as yet. By the same token, though, he should not be openly fearful or terrified by a stranger—and especially should not show any fear of his owner!

In direct contrast, the puppy should not be ridiculously over-active,

A typy seven-week-old puppy exhibiting the heavy wrinkling so desired in the breed. This puppy was bred by Connie Tarrier.

living quarters will have a normal, though spirited, outlook on life and will do its utmost to win you over without having to go into a tailspin.

If the general behavior and appearance of the dog thus far appeal to you, it is time for you to observe him more closely for additional physical requirements. First of all, you cannot expect to find in the puppy the coat he will bear upon maturity. That will come with time and good food and will be additionally enhanced by the many wonderful grooming aids which can be found in pet shops today. Needless to say, the healthy puppy's coat should have a nice shine to it, and the more dense at this age, the better the coat will be when the dog reaches adulthood. Look for clear, sparkling eyes that are free of discharge.

It is important to check the bite. Even though the puppy will cut another complete set of teeth somewhere between four and seven months of age, there will already be some indication of how the final teeth will be positioned.

Puppies take anything and almost everything into their mouths to chew on, and a lot of diseases and infections start or are introduced in the mouth. Brown-stained teeth, for instance, may indicate the puppy has had a past case

either. The puppy that frantically bounds around the room and is never still is not especially desirable. And beware of the "spinners." Spinners are the puppies or dogs that have become neurotic from being kept in cramped quarters or in crates and behave in an emotionally unstable manner when let loose in adequate space. When let out they run in circles and seemingly "go wild." Puppies with this kind of traumatic background seldom ever regain full composure or adjust to the big outside world. The puppy which has had proper exercise and appropriate

of distemper, and the teeth will remain that way. This fact must be reckoned with if you have a show puppy in mind. The puppy's breath should be neither sour nor unpleasant. Bad breath can be a result of a poor food mixture in the diet, or of eating low quality meat, especially if it is fed raw. Some people say that the healthy puppy's breath should have a faint odor that is vaguely reminiscent of garlic. At any rate, a puppy should never be fed just table scraps, but should be raised on a well-balanced diet containing a good dry puppy chow and a good grade of fresh meat. Poor meat and too much cereal or fillers tend to make the puppy grow too fat. Puppies should be in good flesh but not fat from the wrong kind of food.

Needless to say, the puppy should be clean. The breeder that shows a dirty puppy is one to steer away from. Look closely at the skin. Make sure it is not covered with insect bites or red, blotchy sores and dry scales. The vent area around the tail should not show evidences of diarrhea or inflammation. By the same

Two top chocolates, Beaux-Art Chocolate Eclair and Beaux-Art Chocolate Elite. This horse coat brother–sister pair was bred by the Dions.

token, the puppy's fur should not be matted with feces or smell strongly of urine.

True enough, you can wipe dirty eyes, clean dirty ears, and give the puppy a bath when you get it home, but these things are all indications of how the puppy has been cared for during the important formative first months of its life, and they can vitally influence the pup's future health and development. There are many reputable breeders raising healthy puppies that have been reared in proper places and under the proper conditions in clean housing, so why take a chance on a series of veterinary bills and a questionable constitution?

MALE OR FEMALE?

The choice of sex in your puppy is also something that must be given serious thought before you buy. For the pet owner, the sex that would best suit the family life you enjoy would be the paramount choice to consider. For the breeder or exhibitor, there are other vital considerations. If you are looking for a stud to establish a kennel, it is essential that you select a dog with both testicles

Beaux-Art Peaches and Cream and Beaux-Art Golden Nugget. Bred and owned by the Beaux-Art Kennels in Sunrise, FL.

Why the quizzical look? Connie Tarrier's ten-week-old puppy seems to have a question on his mind at the Ce-Te Kennels.

evident, even at a tender age. If there is any doubt, have a vet verify this before the sale is finalized.

The visibility of only one testicle, known as monorchidism, automatically disqualifies the dog from the show ring or from a breeding program, though monorchids are capable of siring. Additionally, it must be noted that monorchids frequently sire dogs with the same deficiency, and to knowingly introduce this into a bloodline is an unwritten sin in the fancy.

Also, a monorchid can sire dogs that are completely sterile. Such dogs are referred to as cryptorchids and have no testicles.

An additional consideration in the male versus female decision for private owners is that with males there might be the problem of leg-lifting and with females there is the inconvenience while they are in heat. However, this need not be the problem it used to be—pet shops sell "pants" for both sexes, which help to control the situation.

Two Ce-Te puppies at seven weeks of age. Bred in 1983 by Connie Tarrier. They are, by name, Hai K'ai and Tien of Paradise.

THE PLANNED PARENTHOOD BEHIND YOUR PUPPY

Never be afraid to ask pertinent questions about the puppy, nor questions about the sire and dam. Feel free to ask the breeder if you might see the dam; the purpose of your visit is to determine her general health and her appearance as a representative of the breed. Also, ask to see the sire, if the breeder is the owner. Ask what the puppy has been fed and should be fed after weaning. Ask to see the pedigree, and inquire if the litter or the individual puppies have been registered with the American Kennel Club, how many of the temporary and/or permanent inoculations the puppy has had, when and if the puppy has been wormed, and whether it has had any illness, disease, or infection.

You need not ask if the puppy is housebroken; it won't mean much. He may have gotten the idea as to where "the place" is where he lives now, but he will need new training to learn where "the place" is in his new home! You can't really expect too much from puppies at this age anyway. Housebreaking is entirely up to the new owner. We know puppies always eliminate when they first awaken and sometimes dribble when they get excited. If friends and relatives are coming over to see the new puppy, make sure he is walked just before he greets them at the front door. This will help.

The normal elimination time for puppies is about every two or three hours. As the time draws near, either take the puppy out or indicate the newspaper for the same purpose. Housebreaking is never easy, but anticipation is about 90 percent of solving the problem. The schools that offer to housebreak your dog are virtually useless. Here again the puppy will learn the place at the schoolhouse, but coming home he will need special training for the new location.

A reputable breeder will welcome any and all questions you might ask and will voluntarily offer additional information, if only to brag about the tedious and loving care he has given the litter. He will also sell a puppy on a 24-hour veterinary approval basis. This means you have a full day to get the puppy to a veterinarian of your choice to get his opinion on the general health of the puppy before you make a final decision. There should also be veterinary certificates and full particulars on the dates and types of inoculations the puppy has been given up to that time.

PUPPIES AND WORMS

Let us give further attention to the unhappy and very unpleasant subject of worms. Generally speaking, most puppies— even those raised in clean quarters—come into contact

Charmer and a Kim Lou puppy at their kennel in Nixa, MO.

with worms early in life. The worms can be passed down from the mother before birth or picked up during the puppies' first encounters with the earth or their kennel facilities. To say that you must not buy a puppy because of an infestation of worms is nonsensical. You might be passing up a fine animal that can be freed of worms in one short treatment, although a heavy infestation of worms of any kind in a young dog is dangerous and debilitating.

The extent of the infection can be readily determined by a veterinarian, and you might take his word as to whether the future health and conformation of the dog has been damaged. He can prescribe the dosage and supply the medication at

this time, and you will already have one of your problems solved.

VETERINARY INSPECTION

While your veterinarian is going over the puppy you have selected, you might just as well ask him for his opinion of it as a breed, as well as the facts about its general health. While few veterinarians can claim to be breed-conformation experts, they usually have a good eye for a worthy specimen and can advise you where to go for further information. Perhaps your veterinarian could also recommend other breeders if you should want another opinion. The veterinarian can point out structural faults or organic problems that affect all breeds and can usually judge whether an animal has been abused or mishandled and whether it is oversized or undersized.

I would like to emphasize here that it is only through this type of close cooperation between owners and veterinarians that we can expect to reap the harvest of modern research.

Most reliable veterinarians are more than eager to learn about various breeds of purebred dogs, and we in turn must acknowledge and apply what they have proved through experience and research in their field. We can buy and breed the best

Shar-Pei puppy displaying the abundant wrinkles characteristic of the breed.

Beaux-Art Florida Snow, a dilute cream horse coat bred and owned by Barbara Dion. Snow is five-weeks-old in this photo.

dog in the world, but when disease strikes we are only as safe as our veterinarian is capable—so let's keep him informed, breed by breed and dog by dog. The veterinarian can mean the difference between life and death!

THE CONDITIONS OF SALE

While it is customary to pay for the puppy before you take it away with you, you should be able to give the breeder a deposit if there is any doubt about the puppy's health. Depending on local laws, you might also postdate a check to cover the 24-four hour veterinary approval. If you decide to take the puppy, the breeder is required to supply you with a pedigree, along with the puppy's registration papers. He is also obliged to supply you with complete information about the inoculations and American Kennel Club instructions on how to transfer ownership of the puppy to your name.

For convenience, some breeders will offer buyers time payment plans if the price on a show dog is very high or if deferred payments are the only way you can purchase the dog. However, any such terms must be worked out between buyer and breeder and should be put in writing to avoid later complications.

You will find most breeders cooperative if they believe you are sincere in your love for the puppy and

Tzo Tzo's Mamie of Tail's End at three months of age. Mamie was a multi-BIS winner as a puppy. The sire was Bigsky's Pretty Boy Floyd Gold ex Kasu's Night Angel of Tzo Tzo. Owner, Ann Coleman.

of the advertising his kennel and bloodlines would receive by your showing the dog in the ring. If you want a pet, buy a pet. Be honest about it, and let the breeder decide on this basis which is the best dog for you. Your conscience will be clear and you'll both be doing a real service to the breed.

BUYING A SHOW PUPPY

If you are positive about breeding and showing, make this point clear so that the breeder will sell you the best possible puppy. If you are dealing with an established kennel, you will have to rely partially, if not entirely, on their choice, since they know their bloodlines and what they can expect from the breeding. They know how their stock develops, and it would be foolish of them to sell you a puppy that could not stand up as a show specimen representing their stock in the ring.

However, you must also realize that the breeder may be keeping the best puppy in the litter to show and breed himself. If this is the case, you might be wise to select the best puppy of the opposite sex so that the dogs will not be competing against one another in the show rings.

THE PURCHASE PRICE

Prices vary on all puppies, of course, but a good show

that you will give it the proper home and the show ring career it deserves (if it is sold as a show-quality specimen of the breed). Remember, when buying a show dog, it is impossible to guarantee what mother nature has created. A breeder can only tell you what he *believes* will develop into a show dog, so be sure your breeder is an honest one.

Also, if you purchase a show prospect and promise to show the dog, you definitely should show it! It is a waste to have a beautiful dog that deserves recognition in the show ring sitting at home as a family pet, and it is unfair to the breeder. This is especially true if the breeder offered you a reduced price because prospect at six weeks to six months of age will usually sell for several hundred dollars. If the puppy is really outstanding, and the pedigree and parentage are also outstanding, the price will be even higher. Honest breeders, however, will all quote around the same figure, so price should not be a strong deciding factor in your choice. If you have any questions as to the current price range, a few telephone calls to different kennels will give you a good average. Reputable breeders will usually stand behind the health of their puppies should something drastically wrong develop. Their obligation to make an adjustment or replacement is usually honored. However, this must be agreed to in writing at the time of the purchase.

Little Courtney Rowley setting up a Shar-Pei puppy in perfect show stance.

Breeding
— Your Shar-Pei —

Let us assume the time has come for your dog to be bred, and you have decided you are in a position to enjoy producing a litter of puppies that you hope will make a contribution to the breed. The bitch you purchased is sound, her temperament is excellent and she is a most worthy representative of the breed.

You have a calendar and have counted off the ten days since the first day of red staining and have determined the tenth to 14th day, which will more than likely be the best period for the actual mating. You have additionally counted off 60 to 65 days before the puppies are likely to be born to make sure everything necessary for their arrival will be in good order by that time.

From the moment the idea of having a litter occurred to you, your thoughts should

have been given to the correct selection of a proper stud. Here again, the novice would do well to seek advice on analyzing pedigrees and tracing bloodlines for the best breedings. As soon as the bitch is in season and you see color (or staining) and a swelling of the vulva, it is time to notify the owner of the stud you selected and make appointments for the breedings. There are several pertinent questions you will want to ask the stud owners after having decided upon the pedigree. The owners, naturally, will also have a few questions they wish to ask you. These questions will concern your bitch's bloodlines, health, age, how many previous litters she's had, if any, and so forth.

GENETICS

No one can guarantee nature! But, with facts and theories at your command

Four-week-old Mo-Ti Fantasia of Beaux-Art. Owners, Ron and Barbara Dion.

his work, he published a paper on his experiments in a scientific journal in the year 1866. That paper went unnoticed for many years, but the laws and theories put forth in it have been tried and proven. Today they are accepted by scientists, as well as dog breeders.

To help understand the Mendelian law as it applies to breeding dogs, we must acquaint ourselves with certain scientific terms and procedures. First of all, dogs possess glands of reproduction which are called gonads. The gonads of the male are in the testicles which produce sperm or spermatozoa. The gonads of the female are the ovaries and produce eggs. The bitch is born with these eggs and, when she is old enough to reproduce, she comes into heat. The eggs descend from the ovaries, via the fallopian tubes into the two horns of the uterus. There they either pass out during the heat cycle or are fertilized by the male sperm in the semen deposited during a mating.

In dog mating, there is what we refer to as a tie, which is a time period during which the male deposits about 600 million spermatozoa into the female to fertilize the ripened eggs. When the sperm and the ripe eggs meet zygotes are created, and the little one-celled future puppies

you can at least, on paper, plan a litter of puppies that should fulfill your fondest expectations. Since the ultimate purpose of breeding is to try to improve the breed, this planning, no matter how uncertain, should be earnestly attempted.

There are a few terms you should be familiar with to help you understand the breeding procedure and the structure of genetics. The first thing that comes to mind is the Mendelian Law— or the Laws of Mendelian Inheritance. Who was Mendel?

Gregor Mendel was an Austrian clergyman and botanist born in Brunn, Moravia. He developed his basic theories on heredity while working with peas. Not realizing the full import of descend from the fallopian tubes into the uterus, where they attach themselves to the walls of the uterus and begin to develop. With all inherited characteristics determined when the zygote was formed, the dam must now assume her role as incubator for her babies, which are organisms in their own right. The bitch has been bred and is now in whelp!

Let us take a closer look at what is happening during the breeding phenomenon. We know that while the male deposits as many as 600 million sperm into the female, the number of ripe eggs she releases will determine the number of puppies in the litter.

Therefore, those breeders who advertise their stud as "producer of large litters" do not know the facts. The bitch determines the size of the litter; the male, the sex of the puppies. It takes only one sperm of the 600 million to produce a puppy.

Each dog and bitch possess 39 pairs of chromosomes in each reproductive germ cell. The chromosomes carry the genes, like peas in a pod, and there are approximately 150,000 genes in each chromosome. These chromosomes split apart and unite with half the chromosomes from the other parent, and the puppy's looks and temperament are created.

A box full of wrinkles: 14-day-old puppies photographed by Barbara Dion at Bill Rous's kennel in Fort Lauderdale, FL.

To understand the procedure more thoroughly, we must understand that there are two kinds of genes—dominant and recessive. A dominant gene is one of a pair whose influence is expressed to the exclusion of the effects of the other. A recessive gene is one of a pair whose influence is subdued by the effects of the other. Most of the important qualities we wish to perpetuate in our breeding programs are carried on by the dominant genes. It is the successful breeder who becomes expert at eliminating recessive or undesirable genes and building up the dominant or desirable ones. This principle holds true in every phase of breeding—inside and outside the dog!

There are many excellent books available which will take you deeper into the fascinating subject of canine genetics. You can learn about your chances of getting so many black, so many white, and so many black and white puppies. etc. Avail yourself of this information before your next, or hopefully, first breeding. I have merely touched upon genetics here to point out the importance of planned parenthood. Any librarian can help you find further information, or books may be purchased offering the very latest findings in canine genetics. It is a fascinating and rewarding field toward creating better dogs.

Barbara Dion and three three-day-old pups, all brush coat creams whelped at her Beaux-Art Kennel.

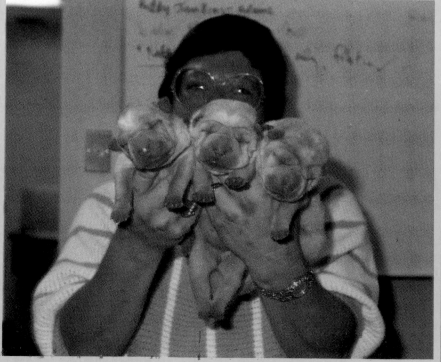

THE POWER IN PEDIGREES

Someone in the dog fancy once remarked that the definition of a show prospect puppy is one third the pedigree, one third what you see and one third what you *hope* it will be! Well, no matter how you break down your qualifying fractions, we all quite agree that good breeding is essential if you have any plans at all for a show career for your dog. Many breeders will buy on pedigree alone, counting largely on what they themselves can do with the puppy by way of feeding, conditioning, and training. Needless to say, that very important piece of paper is reassuring to a breeder or buyer new at the game or to one who has a breeding program in mind and is trying to establish his own bloodline.

One of the most fascinating aspects of tracing pedigrees is the way the names of the really great dogs of the past keep appearing in the pedigrees of the great dogs of today— proof positive of the strong influence of heredity and witness to a great deal of truth in the statement that great dogs frequently reproduce themselves, though not necessarily in appearance only. A pedigree represents something of value when one is dedicated to breeding better dogs.

To the novice buyer or one who is perhaps merely switching to another breed and sees only a frolicking, leggy, squirming bundle of energy in a fur coat, a

Winner of the Stud Dog class at the 1986 Mid-Atlantic Shar-Pei Specialty under judge Richard Tang was Ch. Albright's Eric The Red with Cathi Schneider, pictured with Ch. Lin Choi's Punk-E-Bruzer with Linda Rowleg, and Glimmer Glen's Obsession of Eric with Heather Schneider.

count made to determine just exactly how fertile or potent the stud is. Determine for yourself whether the dog has two normal testicles.

When considering your bitch for this mating, you must take into consideration a few important points that lead to a successful breeding. You and the owner of the stud will want to recall whether she has had normal heat cycles, whether there were too many runts in the litter and whether a Caesarean section was ever necessary. Has she ever had a vaginal infection? Could she take care of her puppies by herself, or was there a milk shortage? How many surviving puppies were there from the litter, and what did they grow up to be in comparison to the requirements of the breed Standard?

Don't buy a bitch that has problems in heat and has never had a live litter. Don't be afraid, however, to buy a healthy maiden bitch, since chances are, if she is healthy and from good stock, she will be a healthy producer. Don't buy a monorchid male, and certainly not a cryptorchid. If there is any doubt in your mind about his potency, get a sperm count from the veterinarian. Older dogs that have been good producers and that are for sale are usually not too hard to find at good,

pedigree can mean everything! To those of us who believe in heredity, a pedigree is more like an insurance policy—so always read it carefully and take heed.

For the more serious breeder who wishes to make a further study of bloodlines in relation to his breeding program, the American Kennel Club library stud books can and should be consulted.

THE BREEDING STOCK

Some of your first questions should concern whether the stud has already proven himself by siring a normal healthy litter. Also inquire as to whether the owners have had a sperm established kennels. If they are not too old and have sired quality show puppies, they can give you some excellent show stock from which to establish your own breeding lines.

The best advice used to be not to breed a bitch until her second heat. Today, with our new scientific knowledge, we have become acutely aware of such things as hip dysplasia, juvenile cataracts, and other congenital diseases. The best advice now seems to be aimed at not breeding your dogs before two years of age, when both the bitch and the sire have been examined by qualified veterinarians and declared, in writing, to be free and clear of these conditions.

The stud fee will vary considerably—the better the bloodlines and the more winning the dog does at shows, the higher the fee. Stud service from a top winning dog could run up to $500. Here again, there may be exceptions. Some breeders will take part cash and then, say, third pick of the litter. The fee can be arranged by a private contract rather than the traditional procedure we have described. Here again, it is wise to get the details of the payment of the stud fee in writing to avoid trouble.

THE DAY OF THE MATING

Now that you have decided upon the proper male and female combination to produce what you hope will be, according to the pedigrees, a fine litter of puppies, it is time to set the date. You have selected the two days (with a one day lapse in

A litter of puppies bred by Cathi Schneider of Glimmer Glen, Sewickley Heights, PA.

between) that you feel are best for the breeding, and you call the owner of the stud. The bitch always goes to the stud, unless, of course, there are extenuating circumstances. You set the date and the time and arrive with the bitch *and* the money.

Standard procedure is payment of a stud fee at the time of the first breeding if there is a tie. For the stud fee, you are entitled to two breedings with ties. Contracts may be written up with specific conditions on breeding terms, of course, but this is general procedure. Often a breeder will take the pick of a litter to protect and maintain his bloodlines. This can be especially desirable if he needs an outcross for his breeding program or if he wishes to continue his own bloodlines, if he sold you the bitch to start with and this mating will continue his

line-breeding program. This should all be worked out ahead of time and written and signed before the two dogs are bred. Remember that the payment of the stud fee is for the services of the stud—not for a guarantee of a litter of puppies. This is why is it so important to make sure you are using a proven stud. Also bear in mind that the American Kennel Club will not register a litter of puppies sired by a male that is under eight months of age. In the case of an older dog, they will not register a litter sired by a dog over 12 years of age, unless there is a witness to the breeding in the form of a veterinarian or other responsible person.

Many studs over 12 years of age are still fertile and capable of producing puppies, but if you do not witness the breeding there is always the danger of a "substitute" stud being used

Multi-BISS Ch. Shir Du Bang repeats a previous win as he takes the 1987 Stud Dog class at the Shar-Pei Club of America Specialty. Handler was Jean Niedermeyer for owners Lawrence and Jackie Bulgin, Show Me Kennels.

to produce a litter. This brings up the subject of sending your bitch away to be bred if you cannot accompany her.

The disadvantages of sending a bitch away to be bred are numerous. First of all, she will not be herself in a strange place, so she'll be difficult to handle. Transportation, if she goes by air (while reasonably safe), is still a traumatic experience. There is always the danger of her being put off at the wrong airport, not being fed or watered properly, and so on.

Some bitches get so upset that they go out of season and the trip—which may prove expensive, especially on top of a substantial stud fee—will have been for nothing.

If at all possible,

accompany your bitch so that the experience is as comfortable for her as it can be. In other words, make sure, before setting this kind of schedule for a breeding, that there is no stud in the area that might be as good for her as the one that is far away. Don't sacrifice the proper breeding for convenience, since bloodlines are so important, but put the safety of the bitch above all else. There is always a risk in traveling, since dogs are considered cargo on a plane.

THE ACTUAL MATING

It is always advisable to muzzle the bitch. A terrified bitch may fear-bite the stud or one of the people involved, and the wild or

Best in Stud Dog class at the 1984 Specialty is multi-BISS Ch. Shir Du Bang of Show Me with Jean Niedermeyer handling and some of his get. Photo by Bruce K. Harkins.

maiden bitch may snap or attack the stud to the point where he may become discouraged and lose interest in the breeding. Muzzling can be done with a lady's stocking tied around the muzzle with a half knot, crossed under the chin and knotted at the back of the neck. There is enough "give" in the stocking for her to breathe or salivate freely and yet not open her jaws far enough to bite. Place her in front of her owner, who holds on to her collar and talks to her and calms her as much as possible.

If the male will not mount on his own initiative, it may be necessary for the owner to assist in lifting him onto the bitch, perhaps even in guiding him to the proper place. The tie is usually accomplished once the male gets the idea. The owner should remain close at hand, however, to make sure the tie is not broken before an adequate breeding has been completed. After a while the stud may get bored and try to break away. This could prove injurious. It may be necessary to hold him in place until the tie is broken.

We must stress at this point that, while some bitches carry on physically and vocally during the tie, there is no way the bitch can be hurt. However, a stud can be seriously or even permanently damaged by a bad breeding. Therefore, the owner of the bitch must be reminded that she must not be alarmed by any commotion. All concentration should be devoted to the stud and to a successful and properly executed service.

Many people believe that breeding dogs is simply a matter of placing two dogs, a male and a female, in close proximity, and letting nature take its course. While this is often true, you cannot count on it. Sometimes it is hard work, and in the case of valuable stock it is essential to supervise to be sure of the safety factor, especially if one or both of the dogs are inexperienced. If the owners are also inexperienced, it may not take place at all.

ARTIFICIAL INSEMINATION

Breeding by means of artificial insemination is usually unsuccessful, unless under a veterinarian's supervision, and can lead to an infection for the bitch and discomfort for the dog. The American Kennel Club requires a veterinarian's certificate to register puppies from such a breeding. Although the practice has been used for over two decades, it now offers new promise, since research has been conducted to make it a more feasible procedure for the future.

Great dogs may eventually look forward to reproducing themselves years after they have left this earth. There now exists a frozen semen concept that has been tested and found successful. The study, headed by Dr. Stephen W.J. Seager, an instructor at the University of Oregon Medical School, has the financial support of the American Kennel Club, indicating that organization's interest in the work. The study is being monitored by the Morris Animal Foundation of Denver, Colorado.

Dr. Seager announced in 1970 that he had been able to preserve dog semen and to produce litters with the stored semen. The possibilities of selective world-wide breedings by this method are exciting. Imagine simply mailing a vial of semen to the bitch! The perfection of line-breeding by storing semen without the threat of death interrupting the breeding program is exciting also.

Dilute cream female at six weeks of age, Mo-Ti Fantasia of Beaux-Art. Bred by Caroline Graham; owners are Ronald and Barbara Dion.

As it stands today, the technique for artificial insemination requires the depositing of semen (taken directly from the dog) into the bitch's vagina, past the cervix and into the uterus by syringe. The correct temperature of the semen is vital, and there is no guarantee of success. The storage method, if successfully adopted, will present a new era in the field of purebred dogs.

THE GESTATION PERIOD

Once the breeding has taken place successfully, the seemingly endless waiting period of about 63 days begins. For the first ten days after the breeding, you do absolutely nothing for the bitch—just spin dreams about the delights you will share with the family when the puppies arrive.

Around the tenth day it is time to begin supplementing the diet of the bitch with vitamins and calcium. We strongly recommend that you take her to your veterinarian for a list of the proper or necessary supplements and the correct amounts of each for your particular bitch. Guesses, which may lead to excesses or insufficiencies, can ruin a litter. For the price of a visit to your veterinarian, you will be confident that you are feeding properly.

The bitch should be free of worms, of course, and if there is any doubt in your mind, she should be wormed before the third week of pregnancy. Your veterinarian will advise you on the necessity of this and proper dosage as well.

PROBING FOR PUPPIES

Far too many breeders are overanxious about whether the breeding "took" and are

A litter bred and owned by Doll Weil.

inclined to feel for puppies or to persuade a veterinarian to radiograph or X-ray their bitches to confirm it. Unless there is reason to doubt the normalcy of a pregnancy, this is risky. Certainly 63 days is not too long to wait, and why risk endangering the litter by probing with your inexperienced hands? Few bitches give no evidence of being in whelp, and there is no need to prove it for yourself by trying to count puppies.

ALERTING YOUR VETERINARIAN

At least a week before the puppies are due, you should telephone your veterinarian and notify him that you expect the litter and give him the date. This way he can make sure that there will be someone available to help, should there be any problems during the whelping. Most veterinarians today have answering services and alternative vets on call when they are not available themselves. Some veterinarians suggest that you call them when the bitch starts labor so that they may further plan their time, should they be needed. Discuss this matter with your veterinarian when you first take the bitch to him for her diet instructions, etc.,

The four-week-old kindergarten crew at Beaux-Art Kennels. All cream brush coat puppies.

Caught napping . . . four-week-old Ce-Te's Fiery Red Iyi was bred by Connie Tarrier.

questioning children, other pets nosing around, or strange adults should be avoided. Many a bitch that has been distracted in this way has been known to devour her young. This can be the horrible result of intrusion into the bitch's privacy. There are other ways of teaching children the miracle of birth, and there will be plenty of time later for the whole family to enjoy the puppies. Let them be born under proper and considerate circumstances.

LABOR

Some litters, and many first litters, do not run the full term of 63 days. Therefore, at least a week before the puppies are actually due and at the time you alert your veterinarian as to their expected arrival, start observing the bitch for signs of the commencement of labor. This will manifest itself in the form of ripples running down the sides of her body that will come as a revelation to her as well. It is most noticeable when she is lying on her side. She will be sleeping a great deal as the arrival date comes closer. If she is sitting or walking about, she will perhaps sit down quickly or squat peculiarly. As the ripples become more frequent, birth time is drawing near, and you would be wise not to leave her. Usually within 24 hours before whelping

and establish the method that will best fit in with his schedule.

Even if this is your first litter, I would advise that you go through the experience of whelping without panicking and calling desperately for the veterinarian. Most animal births are accomplished without complications; you should call for assistance only if you run into trouble.

When having her puppies, your bitch will appreciate as little interference and as few strangers around as possible. A quiet place, with her nest, a single familiar face, and her own instincts are all that is necessary for nature to take its course. An audience of squealing and she will stop eating, and as much as a week before she will begin digging a nest. The bitch should be given something resembling a whelping box with layers of newspaper (black and white only) to make her nest. She will dig more and more as birth approaches, and this is the time to begin making your promise to stop interfering unless your help is specifically required. Some bitches whimper and others are silent, but whimpering does not necessarily indicate trouble.

The sudden gush of green fluid from the bitch indicates that the water or fluid surrounding the puppies has "broken" and that they are about to start down the canal and come into the world. When the water breaks, the birth of the first puppy is imminent. The first puppies are usually born within minutes to half an hour of each other, but a couple of hours between the later ones is not uncommon. If you notice the bitch straining constantly without producing a puppy, or if a puppy remains partially in and partially out for too long, it is cause for concern. Breech births (puppies born feet first instead of head first) can often cause delay or hold things up, and this is

A ten-day-old cream puppy whelped at the Beaux-Art Kennels.

often a problem that requires veterinary assistance.

BREECH BIRTHS

Puppies are normally delivered head first; however, some are presented feet first or in other abnormal positions, and they are referred to as a "breech births." Assistance is often necessary to get the puppy out of the canal, and great care must be taken not

Linda McCloy and Cathi Schneider share ownership of this darling puppy bred by Cathi at Glimmer Glen.

to injure the puppy or the dam.

Aid can be given by grasping the puppy with a piece of turkish toweling and pulling gently during the dam's contractions. Be careful not to squeeze the puppy too hard; merely try to ease it out by moving it gently back and forth. Because even this much delay in delivery may mean the puppy is drowning, do not wait for the bitch to

remove the sac. Do it yourself by tearing the sac open to expose the face and head. Then cut the cord anywhere from one-half to three-quarters of an inch away from the navel. If the cord bleeds excessively, pinch the end of it with your fingers and count five. Repeat if necessary. Then pry open the mouth with your finger and hold the puppy upside down for a moment to drain any fluid from the lungs. Next, rub the puppy briskly with turkish or paper toweling. You should get it wriggling and whimpering by this time.

If the litter is large, this assistance will help conserve the strength of the bitch and will probably be welcomed by her. However, it is best to allow her to take care of at least the first few herself to preserve the natural instinct and to provide the nutritive values obtained by her consumption of one or more of the afterbirths as nature intended.

Occasionally the sac will break before the delivery of a puppy and will be expelled while the puppy remains inside, thereby depriving the dam of the necessary lubrication to expel the puppy normally. Inserting vaseline or mineral oil via your finger will help the puppy pass down the birth canal. This is why it is essential that you be present during the whelping so that you can count puppies and afterbirths and determine when and if assistance is needed.

CAESAREAN SECTION

Should the whelping reach the point where there is complication, such as the bitch's not being capable of whelping the puppies herself, the "moment of truth" is upon you and a Caesarean section may be necessary. The bitch may be too small or too immature to expel the puppies herself, her cervix may fail to dilate enough to allow the young to come down the birth canal, there may be torsion of the uterus, a dead or monster puppy, a sideways puppy blocking the canal, or perhaps toxemia. A Caesarean section will be the only solution. No matter what the cause, get the bitch to the veterinarian immediately to insure your chances of saving the mother and/or the puppies.

The Caesarean section operation (the name derived from the idea that Julius Caesar was delivered by this method) involves the removal of the unborn young from the uterus of the dam by surgical incision into the walls through the abdomen. The operation is performed when it has been determined that for some reason the puppies cannot be delivered normally. While modern surgical methods have made the operation itself reasonably safe, with the dam being perfectly capable of nursing the puppies shortly after the completion of the surgery, the chief task lies in the ability to spark life into the puppies immediately upon

A magnificent eight-week-old litter of puppies bred by Doll Weil. The sire was Chico's Roro II ex Albright's Mi-Chu.

their removal from the womb. If the mother dies, the time element is even more important in saving the young, since the oxygen supply ceases upon the death of the dam, and the difference between life and death is measured in seconds.

After surgery, when the bitch is home in her whelping box with the babies, she will probably nurse the young without distress. You must be sure that the sutures are kept clean and that no redness or swelling or ooze appears in the wound. Healing will take place naturally, and no salves or ointments should be applied, unless prescribed by the veterinarian, for fear the puppies will get it into their systems. If there is any doubt, check the bitch for fever, restlessness (other than the natural concern for her young), or a lack of appetite, but do not anticipate trouble.

Even though most dogs are generally easy whelpers, any number of reasons might occur to cause the bitch to have a difficult birth. Before automatically resorting to Caesarean section, many veterinarians are now trying the technique known as episiotomy.

Used rather frequently in human deliveries, episiotomy (pronouced e-pease-e-ott-o-me) is the cutting of the membrane between the rear opening of the vagina back almost to the opening of the anus. After delivery it is stitched together, and barring complications, heals easily, presenting no problem in future births.

FALSE PREGNANCY

The disappointment of a false pregnancy is almost as bad for the owner as it is for the bitch. She goes through the gestation period with all the symptoms—swollen stomach, increased appetite, swollen nipples—and even makes a nest when the time comes. You may even take an oath that you noticed the ripples on her body from the labor pains. Then, just as suddenly as you made up your mind that she was definitely going to deliver puppies, you will know that she definitely is

Future Ch. Chu'd Slipper of Albright, bred and owned by Doll Weil.

not! She may walk around carrying a toy as if it were a puppy for a few days, but she will soon be back to normal and will act as if nothing happened—and nothing did!

FEEDING THE BITCH BETWEEN BIRTHS

Usually the bitch will not be interested in food for about 24 hours before the arrival of the puppies, and perhaps as long as two or three days after their arrival. The placenta that she cleans up after each puppy is high in food value and will be more than ample to sustain her. This is nature's way of allowing the mother to feed herself and her babies without having to leave the nest and hunt for food during the first crucial days. In the wild, the mother always cleans up all traces of birth so as not to attract other animals to her newborn babies.

However, there are those of us who believe in making food available should the mother feel the need to restore her strength during or after delivery—especially if she whelps a large litter. Raw chopped meat, beef bouillon, and milk are all acceptable and may be placed near the whelping box during the first two or three days. After that, the mother will begin to put the babies on a sort of schedule. She will leave the whelping box at frequent intervals, take longer exercise periods and begin

Three four-week-old litter mates bred at Beaux-Art.

157

to take interest in other things. This is where the fun begins for you. Now the babies are no longer soggy little pinkish blobs. They begin to crawl around and squeal and hum and grow before your very eyes!

It is at this time, if all has gone normally, that the family can be introduced gradually and great praise and affection given to the mother.

THE TWENTY-FOUR HOUR CHECKUP

It is smart to have a veterinarian check the mother and her puppies within 24 hours after the last puppy is born. The veterinarian can check the puppies for cleft palates or umbilical herniae and may wish to give the dam—particularly if she is a show dog—an injection of Pituitin to make sure of the expulsion of all afterbirths and to tighten up the uterus. This can prevent a sagging belly after the puppies are weaned when the bitch is being readied for the show ring.

REARING THE FAMILY

Needless to say, even with a small litter there will be certain considerations that must be adhered to in order to insure successful rearing of the puppies. For instance, the diet for the mother should be appropriately increased as the puppies grow and take more and more nourishment from her. During the first few days of rest, while the bitch looks over her puppies and regains her strength, she should be left pretty much alone. It is during these first days that she begins to put the puppies on a feeding schedule and feels safe enough about them to leave the whelping box long enough to take a little extended exercise.

It is cruel, however, to try to keep the mother away from the puppies any longer than she wants to be because you feel she is being too attentive or to give the neighbors a chance to peek in at the puppies. The mother should not have to worry about harm coming to her puppies for the first few weeks. The veterinary checkup will be enough of an experience for her to have to endure until she is more like herself again.

A show puppy prospect should be outgoing (probably the first one to fall out of the whelping box!), and all efforts should be made to socialize the puppy that appears to be the most shy. Once the puppies are about three weeks old, they can and should be handled a great deal by friends and members of the family.

During the third week the puppies begin to try to walk instead of crawl, but they are unsteady on their feet. Tails are used for balancing, and they begin to make sounds.

The crucial period in a puppy's life occurs when the puppy is from 21 to 28 days old, so all the time you can devote to them at this time will reap rewards later on in life. This is the age when several other important steps must be taken in a puppy's life. Weaning should start if it hasn't already, and this is the time to check for worms. Do not worm unnecessarily. A veterinarian should advise on worming and appropriate dosage and he can also discuss with you at this time the schedule for serum or vaccination, which will depend on the size of the puppies as well as their age.

Exercise and grooming should be started at this time, with special care and consideration being given to the diet. You will find that the dam will help you wean the puppies, leaving them alone more and more as she notices that they are eating well on their own. Begin by leaving them with her during the night for comfort and warmth; eventually, when she shows less interest, keep them separated entirely.

By the time the fifth week arrives, you will already be in love with every member of the litter and desperately searching for reasons to keep them all. They recognize you—which really gets to you and they box and chew on each other, try to eat your finger, and have

Shar-Pei make patient and consistent mothers. Young litter napping and feeding with mom. Breeder, Cathi Schneider.

Two puppies bred by Doll Weil at her Doll Acres Farm in Pittsburgh, PA. They are Doll's Philadelphia Cream Cheese and Glimmer Glen's Decadence Doll.

protection that must be afforded a purebred quality bitch can be most worthwhile—even if it is only until a single litter is produced after the first heat. It is then not too late to spay; the progeny can perpetuate the bloodline, the bitch will have been fulfilled—though it is merely an old wives' tale that bitches should have at least one litter to be "normal"— and she may then be retired to her deserved role as family pet once again.

With spaying, the problem of staining and unusual behavior around the house is eliminated, as is the necessity of having to keep her in "pants" or administering pills, sprays, or shots, of which most veterinarians do not approve anyway.

In the case of males, castration is seldom contemplated, which to me is highly regrettable. The owners of male dogs overlook the dog's ability to populate an entire neighborhood, since they do not have the responsibility of rearing and disposing of the puppies. When you take into consideration the many females the male dog can impregnate, it is almost more essential that the males rather than the females be taken out of circulation. The male dog will still be inclined to roam but will be less frantic about leaving the grounds, and you will find that a lot of *wanderlust* has left him.

When considering the problem of spaying or castrating, the first consideration after the population explosion should actually be the health of the dog or bitch. Males are frequently subject to urinary diseases, and sometimes castration is a help. Your veterinarian can best advise you on this problem. Another aspect to consider is the kennel dog that is no longer being used at stud. It is unfair to keep him in a kennel with females in heat when there is no chance for him to be used. There are other, more personal, considerations for both kennel and one-dog owners, but when making the decision, remember that it is final. You can always spay or castrate, but once the deed is done there is no return.

Cat-napping are two Show Me Shar-Pei puppies owned and bred by Lawrence and Jackie Bulgin.

Feeding
— and Nutrition —

FEEDING PUPPIES

There are many diets today for young puppies, including all sorts of products on the market for feeding the newborn, for supplemental feeding of the young, and for adding "this or that" to diets, depending on what is lacking in the way of a complete diet.

When weaning puppies it is necessary to put them on four meals a day, even while you are tapering off with the mother's milk. Feeding at six in the morning, noontime, six in the evening, and midnight is about the best schedule since it fits in with most human eating plans. Meals for the puppies can be prepared immediately before or after your own meals without too much of a change in your own schedule.

Two meat and two milk meals serve best and should be served alternately, of course. Assuming the six a.m. feeding is a milk meal, the contents should be as follows: dilute two parts evaporated milk and one part water along with raw egg yolk, honey or Karo syrup, sprinkled with high-protein baby cereal and wheat germ. Goat's milk is the very best milk to feed puppies but is expensive and usually available only at drug stores, unless you live in farm country where it may be readily available fresh and less expensive. If goat's milk is not available, use evaporated milk (which can be changed to powdered milk later on). As the

A Ben Ching puppy poses in the yard in Cliffwood, NJ.

puppies mature, cottage cheese may be added or, at one of the two milk meals, it can be substituted for the cereal.

At noon, a puppy chow that has been soaked in warm water or beef broth (according to the time specified on the wrapper) should be mixed with raw or simmered chopped meat in equal proportions with vitamin powder added.

At six p.m. repeat the milk meal—perhaps varying the type of cereal from wheat to oats, corn, or rice.

At midnight, repeat the meat meal. If raw meat was fed at noon, the evening meal might be simmered.

Please note that specific proportions on this suggested diet are not given; however, it's safe to say that the most important ingredients are the milk and cereal, and the meat and puppy chow that form the basis of the diet. Your veterinarian can advise on the portion sizes if there is any doubt in your mind as to how much to use.

If you notice that the puppies are cleaning their plates, you are perhaps not feeding enough to keep up with their rate of growth. Increase the amount at the next feeding. Observe them closely; puppies should each "have their fill," because growth is very rapid at this age. If they have not satisfied themselves, increase the amount so that they do not have to fight for the last morsel. They will not overeat if they know there is enough food available. Instinct will usually let them eat to suit their normal capacity.

If there is any doubt in your mind as to any ingredient you are feeding, ask yourself, "Would I give it to my own baby?" If the answer is no, then don't give it to your puppies. At this age, the comparison between puppies and human babies can be a good guide. If there is any doubt in your mind, ask your veterinarian in order to be sure.

Many puppies will regurgitate their food, perhaps a couple of times, before they manage to retain it. If they do bring up their food, allow them to eat it again, rather than clean it away. Sometimes additional saliva is necessary for them to digest it, and you do not want them to skip a meal just because it is an unpleasant sight for you to observe.

This same regurgitation process sometimes holds true with the bitch, who will bring up her own food for her puppies every now and then. This is a natural instinct on her part that stems from the days when dogs were giving birth in the wild. The only food the mother could provide at weaning time was too rough and indigestible for her puppies; therefore, she took it upon herself to predigest the food until it could be taken and retained by her young. Bitches today will sometimes resort to this, especially bitches that love having litters and have a strong maternal instinct. Some dams will help you wean their litters and even give up feeding entirely once they see you are taking over.

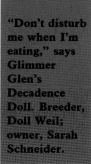

"Don't disturb me when I'm eating," says Glimmer Glen's Decadence Doll. Breeder, Doll Weil; owner, Sarah Schneider.

WEANING PUPPIES

When weaning the puppies, the mother is kept away from the little ones for longer and longer periods of time. This is done over a period of several days. At first she is separated from the puppies for several hours, then all day, staying with them only at night for comfort and warmth. This separation aids in helping the mother's milk to dry up gradually, and she suffers less distress after feeding a litter.

If the mother continues to carry a great deal of milk with no signs of its tapering off, consult your veterinarian before she gets too uncomfortable. She may cut the puppies off from her supply of milk too abruptly if she is uncomfortable; this may occur before they should be completely on their own.

There are many opinions on the proper age to start weaning puppies. If you plan to start selling them between six and eight weeks, weaning should begin between two and three weeks of age. (Here again, each bitch will pose a different situation.) The size and weight of the litter should help determine the time, and your veterinarian will have an opinion as he determines the burden the bitch is carrying by the size of the litter and her general condition. If she is being pulled down by feeding a large litter, he may suggest that you start at two weeks. If she is glorying in her motherhood without any

Eight-day-old puppies bred and owned by Cathi Schneider.

apparent taxing of strength, he may suggest three to four weeks. You and he will be the best judges. But remember, there is no substitute that is as perfect as mother's milk—and the longer the puppies benefit from it, the better. Other food helps, but mother's milk first and foremost makes the healthiest puppies.

ORPHANED PUPPIES

The ideal solution to feeding orphaned puppies is to put them with another nursing dam who will take them on as her own. If this is not possible within your own kennel, or a kennel that you know of, it is up to you to care for and feed the puppies. Survival is possible but requires a great deal of

time and effort on your part.

Your substitute formula must be precisely prepared, always served heated to body temperature, and refrigerated when not being fed. Esbilac, a vacuum-packed powder with complete feeding instructions on the can, is excellent and about as close to mother's milk as you can get. If you can't get Esbilac, or until you do get Esbilac, there are two alternative formulas that you might use.

Mix one part boiled water with five parts evaporated milk and add one teaspoonful of dicalcium phosphate per quart of formula. Dicalcium phosphate can be secured at any drug store. If they have it in tablet form only, you

Mother and baby, Ch. Paradise Co-C's A-Lot Ce-Te and her five-day-old offspring, Ce-Te Chocolate Hui Bing Low. Bred and owned by Connie Tarrier.

can powder the tablets with the back part of a tablespoon. The other formula for newborn puppies is a combination of eight ounces of homogenized milk mixed well with two egg yolks.

You will need baby bottles with three-hole nipples. Sometimes doll bottles can be used for the newborn puppies, which should be fed at six-hour intervals. If they are consuming sufficient amounts, their stomachs should look full, or slightly enlarged, though never distended. The amount of formula to be fed is proportionate to the size, age, growth, and weight of the puppy, and is indicated on the can of Esbilac; or consult your veterinarian if necessary. Many breeders like to keep a baby scale nearby to check the weight of the puppies to be sure they are thriving on the formula.

At two to three weeks you can start adding pablum or some other high protein baby cereal to the formula. Also, baby beef can be licked from your finger at this age, or added to the formula. At four weeks the surviving puppies should be taken off the diet of Esbilac and put on a more substantial diet, such as wet puppy meal or chopped beef; however, Esbilac powder can still be mixed in with the food for additional nutrition. Baby foods of pureed meats in jars also make for a smooth changeover, and can be blended into the diet.

Barbara Dion's five-week-old Fantasia of Beaux-Art.

HOW TO FEED THE NEWBORN PUPPIES

When the puppy is a newborn, remember that it is vitally important to keep the feeding procedure as close to the natural mother's routine as possible. The newborn puppy should be held in your lap in your hand in an almost upright position with the bottle at an angle to allow the entire nipple area to be full of the formula. Do not hold the bottle upright so the puppy's head has to reach straight up toward the ceiling. Do not let the puppy nurse too quickly or take in too much air; this may cause colic. Once in awhile take the bottle away and let him rest a moment and swallow several times. Before feeding, test the nipple to see that the fluid does not come out too quickly, or by the same token, too slowly so that the puppy gets tired of feeding before he has had enough to eat.

When the puppy is a little older, you can place him on his stomach on a towel to eat, and even allow him to hold on to the bottle or to "come and get it" on his own. Most puppies enjoy eating and this will be a good indication of how strong an appetite he has and his ability to consume the contents of the bottle.

It will be necessary to "burp" the puppy. Place a

Beaux-Art Peaches and Cream at two months of age. This cream brush coat was bred and owned by Ron and Barbara Dion.

towel on your shoulder and hold the puppy on your shoulder as if he were a human baby, patting and rubbing him gently. This will also encourage the puppy to defecate. At this time, you should look for diarrhea or other intestinal disorders. The puppy should eliminate after each feeding, with occasional eliminations between times as well. If the puppies do not eliminate on their own after each meal, massage their stomachs and under their tails gently until they do.

You must keep the puppies clean. Under no circumstances should fecal matter be allowed to collect on their skin or fur.

All this, plus your determination and perseverance, might save an entire litter of puppies that would otherwise have died without their real mother.

FEEDING THE ADULT DOG

The puppies' schedule of four meals a day should drop to three by six months and then to two by nine months; by the time the dog reaches one year of age, it is eating one meal a day.

The time when you feed the dog each day can be a matter of the dog's preference or your convenience, so long as once in every 24 hours the dog receives a meal that provides it with a complete, balanced diet. In addition, of course, fresh clean water should be available at all times.

There are many brands of dry food, kibbles, and biscuits on the market that are all of good quality. There are also many varieties of canned dog food that provide a balanced diet for your dog. But for those breeders and exhibitors who show their dogs, additional care is given to providing a few "extras" that enhance the good health and appearance of show dogs.

A good meal or kibble mixed with water or beef broth and raw meat is perhaps the best ration to provide. In cold weather, many breeders add suet or corn oil (or even olive or cooking oil) to the mixture, and others make use of the bacon fat after breakfast by pouring it over the dog's food.

Salting a dog's food in the summer helps replace the

This basketful of Beaux-Art puppies illustrates the various colors which are found in the breed.

173

salt "panted away" in the heat. Many breeders sprinkle the food with garlic powder to sweeten the dog's breath and prevent gas, especially in breeds that gulp or wolf their food and swallow a lot of air. I prefer garlic powder; the salt is too weak and the clove is too strong.

There are those, of course, who cook very elaborately for their dogs, which is not necessary if a good meal and meat mixture is provided. Many prefer to add vegetables, rice, tomatoes, etc., to everything else they feed. As

long as the extras do not throw the nutritional balance off, there is little harm, but no one thing should be fed to excess. Occasionally, liver is given as a treat at home. Fish, which most veterinarians no longer recommend even for cats, is fed to puppies, but should not be given in excess of once a week. Always remember that no one food should be given as a total diet. Balance is most important; a 100% meat diet can kill a dog.

THE ALL-MEAT DIET CONTROVERSY

In March 1971 the National Research Council investigated a great stir in the dog fancy about the all-meat dog-feeding controversy. It was established that meat and meat by-products constitute a complete balanced diet for dogs only when it is further fortified.

Therefore, a good dog chow or meal mixed with meat provides the perfect

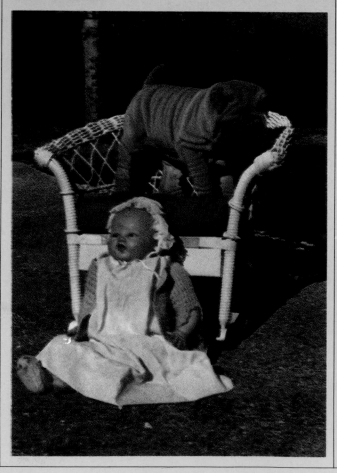

Top: Fun amongst the flowers. Homebred of Zella Llewellyn of Shoestring Acres. *Bottom:* Ce-Te Tien of Paradise at seven weeks of age. Connie Tarrier, breeder.

combination for a dog's diet. While the dry food is a complete diet in itself, the fresh meat additionally satisfies the dog's anatomically and physiologically meat-oriented appetite. While dogs are actually carnivores, it must be remembered that when they were feeding themselves in the wild they ate almost the entire animal they captured, including its stomach contents. This provided some of the vitamins and minerals we must now add to the diet.

In the United States, the Standard for diets that claim to be "complete and balanced" is set by the Subcommittee on Canine Nutrition of the National Research Council (NRC) of the National Academy of Sciences. This is the official agency for establishing the nutritional requirements of dog foods. Most foods sold for dogs and cats meet these requirements and manufacturers are proud to

Adorable puppy at three months of age. This brown horse coat was bred by Peter Belmont and is co-owned by Ronald and Barbara Dion. His name is Temple Toi Tepenyaki.

say so on their labels, so look for this when you buy. Pet food labels must be approved by the Association of American Feed Control Officials (AAFCO) Pet Foods Committee. Both the Food and Drug Administration and the Federal Trade Commission of the AAFCO define the word "balanced" when referring to dog food as follows:

"Balanced is a term which may be applied to pet food having all known required nutrients in a proper amount and proportion based upon the recommendations of a recognized authority (the National Research Council is one) in the field of animal nutrition, for a given set of physiological animal requirements."

With this much care given to your dog's diet, there can be little reason for not having happy, well-fed dogs in proper weight and proportions for the show ring.

OBESITY

As we mentioned before, there are many "perfect" diets for your dogs on the market today. When fed in proper proportions, they should keep your dogs in "full bloom." However, there are those owners who, more often than not, indulge their own appetites and are inclined to overfeed their dogs as well. A study in Great Britain in the early 1970s found that a major percentage of obese people also had obese dogs. The entire family was overfed

Top: Mary Jo Reynolds's Glimmer Glen's Bang-aroo.
Bottom: Glimmer Glen's Elrod of Bang, bred by Cathi Schneider.

and all suffered from the same condition.

Obesity in dogs is a direct result of the animal's being fed more food that he can properly "burn up" over a period of time, so it is stored as fat or fatty tissue in the body. Pet dogs are more inclined to become obese than show dogs or working dogs, but obesity also is a factor to be considered with the older dog since his exercise is curtailed.

A lack of "tuck up" on a dog or not being able to feel the ribs, or great folds of fat that hang from the underside of the dog can all be considered as signs of obesity. Genetic factors may enter into the picture, but usually the owner is at fault.

The life span of the obese dog is decreased on several counts. Excess weight puts undue stress on the heart as well as on the joints. The dog becomes a poor anesthetic risk and has less resistance to viral or bacterial infections. Treatment is seldom easy or completely effective, so emphasis should be placed on not letting your dog get fat in the first place!

GASTRIC TORSION

Gastric torsion or bloat, sometimes referred to as "twisted stomach," has become more and more prevalent. Many dogs that in the past had been thought to die of blockage of the stomach or intestines, because they had swallowed toys or other foreign objects, are now suspected of having been the victims of gastric torsion and the

Beaux-Art Chocolate Elite at three months of age.

Mo-Ti's Lushi of Beaux-Art at seven weeks of age.

bloat that followed.

Though life can be saved by immediate surgery to untwist the organ, the rate of fatality is high. Symptoms of gastric torsion are unusual restlessness, excessive salivation, attempts to vomit, rapid respiration, pain, and the eventual bloating of the abdominal region.

The cause of gastric torsion can be attributed to overeating, excess gas formation in the stomach, poor function of the stomach or intestine, or general lack of exercise. As the food ferments in the stomach, gases form which may twist the stomach in a clockwise direction so that the gas is unable to escape. Surgery, where the stomach is untwisted counter-clockwise, is the safest and most successful way to correct the situation.

To avoid the threat of gastric torsion, it is wise to keep your dog well exercised to be sure the body is functioning normally. Make sure that food and water are available for the dog at all times, thereby reducing the tendency to overeat. With self-service dry feeding, where the dog is able to eat intermittently during the day, there is not the urge to "stuff" at one time.

If you notice any of the symptoms of gastric torsion, call your veterinarian immediately. Death can result within a matter of hours!

Your Dog, Your Veterinarian — and You —

The purpose of this chapter is to explain why you should never attempt to be your own veterinarian. Quite to the contrary, we urge emphatically that you establish good liaison with a reputable veterinarian who will help you maintain happy, healthy dogs. Our purpose is to bring you up-to-date on the discoveries made in modern canine medicine and to help you work with your veterinarian by applying these new developments to your own animals. If you know a little something about the diseases and how to recognize their symptoms, your chances of catching them in the preliminary stages will help you and your veterinarian effect a cure before a serious condition develops.

Your general knowledge of diseases, their symptoms, and side effects will assist your veterinarian. In making a quicker, more accurate diagnosis. He does not expect you to be an expert, but will appreciate your efforts in getting a sick dog to him before it is too late and he cannot save its life.

ACUSCOPING

We are not fully aware of all the remarkable results of acupuncture, but we now hear of a new device called the Acuscope. The Acuscope combines the principles of both acupuncture and biofeedback. This electronically operated tool stimulates an animal's nerves with electricity to reduce stress and pain, and it actually accelerates healing.

Opposite: Cassie's Mr. Perfect, bred by Janie Mancill, Houston, TX, and co-owned by the Dions.

Early show training for Chop Sooy Looy Jr, owned by Cathi Schneider and Linda McCloy.

A veterinarian in California has been using this device since 1984, based on the pioneering efforts of an upstate New York physician who developed it over a decade ago. It might be a good idea to mention it to your own veterinarian if you find that current methods of treatment are not working to your satisfaction.

CARDIOPULMONARY RESUSCITATION FOR DOGS

There has been a lot of discussion regarding the CPR process of restoring breath to animals. With large dogs, the same procedures can be used as with a human—and I hope all of you know CPR for humans! With small dogs, instead of blows you use "puffs" of air to restore breathing. Briefly, these are the steps: determine unresponsiveness, call for help, open the mouth, look, listen and feel for breathing, check pulse. Breathe for the dog once every three to five seconds. If further aid is required, use 15 chest compressions to every two breaths, or four to six times per minute. If the dog is choking, use four back blows, four abdominal thrusts, or pushes *up under* the rib cage. Check before repeating the cycle of thrusts and blows. Telephone for help and/or transport to the veterinarian immediately. It would be wise to post a diagram of instructions in your kennel room, and to educate all members of your family to this procedure. It could make the difference between life and death.

ASPIRIN USAGE

There is a common joke about doctors telling their patients, when they telephone with a complaint, to take an aspirin, go to bed and let him know how things are in the morning. Unfortunately, that is exactly the way it turns out with a lot of dog owners who think aspirins are cure-alls and give them to their dogs

Beaux-Art's Red Hot Lover, four-month-old red brush coat, bred and owned by Beaux-Art Kennels.

indiscriminately. They finally call the veterinarian when the dog has an unfavorable reaction.

Aspirins are not panaceas for everything—certainly not for every dog. In an experiment, fatalities in cats treated with aspirin in one laboratory alone numbered ten out of 13 within a two-week period. Dogs' tolerance was somewhat better as to actual fatalities, but there was considerable evidence of ulceration on the stomach linings in varying degrees when necropsy was performed.

Aspirin has been held in the past to be almost as effective for dogs as for people when given for many of the everyday aches and pains. The fact remains, however, that medication of any kind should be administered only after veterinary consultation and after a specific dosage suitable to the condition is recommended.

While aspirin is chiefly effective in reducing fever, relieving minor pains, and cutting down on inflammation, the acid has been proven harmful to the stomach when given in strong doses. Only your veterinarian is qualified to determine what the dosage is or whether it should be administered to your particular dog at all.

USING A THERMOMETER

You will notice in reading this chapter dealing with the diseases of dogs that practically everything a dog might contract in the way of sickness has basically the same set of symptoms: loss of appetite, diarrhea, dull eyes, dull coat, warm and/or runny nose and *fever!*

Therefore, it is most

Ch. Doll's Pretty Prunella truly lives up to her name. Bred by Doll Weil and owned by Mary Concialdi. The sire was Ch. Glimmer Glen's Chop Sooy Looy ex Ch. Albright's Ugli Ermi.

advisable to have a thermometer on hand for checking temperature. There are several inexpensive metal, rectal-type thermometers that are accurate and safer than the glass variety that can be broken. Breakage may occur either by dropping it or perhaps by its breaking off in the dog because of improper insertion or an aggravated condition with the dog that makes him violently resist the insertion of the thermometer.

Whatever type you use, it should first be sterilized with alcohol and then lubricated with petroleum jelly to make the insertion as easy as possible.

The normal temperature for a dog is 101.5 ° Fahrenheit, as compared to the human 98.6 °. Excitement as well as illness can cause this to vary a degree or two, but any sudden or extensive rise in body temperature must be considered as cause for alarm. Your first indication will be that your dog feels unduly "warm" and this is the time to take the temperature, *not* when the dog becomes very ill or manifests additional serious symptoms. With a thermometer on hand, you can check temperature quickly and perhaps prevent some illnesses from becoming serious.

The line-up at Beaux-Art Kennels. Swing C'mork and sons Sampson and Red Hot Lover.

185

Temple Toi Tasmin, owned by Lisa Berns, Davie, FL.

COPROPHAGY

Perhaps the most unpleasant of all phases of dog breeding is to come up with a dog that takes to eating stool. This practice, which is referred to politely as coprophagy, is one of the unsolved mysteries in the dog world. There simply is no confirmed explanation as to why some dogs do it.

However, there are several logical theories, all or any of which may be the cause. Some people cite nutritional deficiencies; others say that dogs that are inclined to gulp their food (which passes through them not entirely digested) find it still partially palatable. There is another theory that the preservatives used in some meat are responsible for an appealing odor that remains through the digestive process. Then again, poor quality meat can be so tough and unchewable that dogs swallow it whole and it passes through them in large undigested chunks.

There are others who believe the habit is strictly psychological, the result of a nervous condition or insecurity. Others believe the dog cleans up after itself because it is afraid of being punished as it was when it made a mistake on the carpet as a puppy. Some people claim boredom is the reason, or even spite. Others will tell you a dog does not want its personal odor on the premises for fear of attracting other hostile animals to itself or its home.

The most logical of all explanations and the one veterinarians are inclined to accept is that it is a deficiency of dietary enzymes. Too much dry food can be bad and many veterinarians suggest trying meat tenderizers, monosodium glutamate, or garlic powder, all of which give the stool a bad odor and discourage the dog. Yeast, certain vitamins, or a complete change of diet are even more often suggested. By the time you try each of the above you will probably discover that the dog has outgrown the habit anyway.

However, the condition cannot be ignored if you are to enjoy your dog to the fullest.

There is no set length of time that the problem persists, and the only real cure is to walk the dog on leash, morning and night and after every meal. In other words, set up a definite eating and exercising schedule before coprophagy is an established pattern.

MASTURBATION

A source of embarrassment to many dog owners, masturbation can be eliminated with a minimum of training.

The dog that is constantly

Will the real Shar-Pei please stand up! It's the one in the middle, Lushi owned by the Dions.

187

breeding anything and everything, including the leg of the piano or perhaps the leg of your favorite guest, can be broken of the habit by stopping its cause.

The over-sexed dog, if truly that is what he is, which will never be used for breeding can be castrated. The kennel stud dog can be broken of the habit by removing any furniture from his quarters or keeping him on leash and on verbal command when he is around people or in the house where he might be tempted to breed pillows, people, etc.

Hormonal imbalance may be another cause and your veterinarian may advise injections. Exercise can be of tremendous help.

Keeping the dog's mind occupied by physical play when he is around people will also help relieve the situation.

Females might indulge in sexual abnormalities like masturbation during their heat cycle, or, again, because of a hormonal imbalance. But if they behave this way because of a more serious problem, a hysterectomy may be indicated.

A sharp "no" command when you can anticipate the act, or a sharp "no" when caught in the act will deter most dogs if you are consistent in your correction. Hitting or other physical abuse will only confuse a dog.

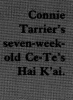

Connie Tarrier's seven-week-old Ce-Te's Hai K'ai.

Impressive headstudy of Sunshines Sally Yun Yang, owned by the Ben Ching Kennels of Vivien and Charlie Kelly, Cliffwood, NJ.

RABIES

The greatest fear in the dog fancy today is still the great fear it has always been—rabies.

What has always held true about this dreadful disease still holds true today. The only way rabies can be contracted is through the saliva of a rabid animal entering the bloodstream of another animal or person. There is, of course, the Pasteur treatment for rabies which is very effective.

It should be administered immediately if there is any question of exposure. There was of late the incident of a little boy who survived being bitten by a rabid bat. Even more than dogs being found to be rabid, we now know that the biggest carriers are bats, skunks, foxes, rabbits, and other warmblooded animals that pass it from one to another since they do not have the benefit of inoculation. Dogs that run free should be inoculated for protection against these animals. For city or house dogs that never leave their owner's side, it may not be as necessary.

For many years, Great Britain (because it is an island and because of the country's strictly enforced six-month quarantine) was entirely free of rabies. But in 1969 a British officer brought back his dog from foreign duty and the dog was found to have the disease soon after being

A typical typy puppy bred at the Shoestring Acres Kennels in Alvin, TX.

released from quarantine. There was a great uproar about it, with Britain killing off wild and domestic animals in a great scare campaign, but the quarantine is once again down to six months and things seem to have returned to a normal, sensible attitude.

Health departments in rural towns usually provide rabies inoculations free of charge. If your dog is outdoors a great deal or exposed to other animals that are, you might wish to call the town hall and get information on the program in your area. One cannot be too cautious about this dread disease. While the number of cases diminishes each year, there are still thousands being reported and there is still the constant threat of an outbreak where animals roam free. Never forget that there is no cure.

Rabies is caused by a neurotropic virus which can be found in the saliva, brain, and sometimes the blood of the afflicted warmblooded animal. The incubation period is from two weeks to six months, which means you can be exposed to it without any visible symptoms. As we have said, while there is still no known cure, it can be controlled.

You can help effect this control by reporting animal

bites and by educating the public on the dangers, symptoms, and prevention, so that we may reduce the fatalities.

There are two kinds of rabies; one form is called "furious" and the other is referred to as "dumb." The mad dog goes through several stages of the disease. His disposition and behavior change radically and suddenly; he becomes irritable and vicious. The eating habits alter, and he rejects food for things like stones and sticks; he becomes exhausted and drools saliva out of his mouth constantly. He may hide in corners, look glassy-eyed and suspicious, bite at the air as he races around snarling and attacking with his tongue hanging out. At this point paralysis sets in, starting at the throat so that he can no longer drink water though he desires it desperately; hence, the term hydrophobia is given. He begins to stagger and eventually to convulse, and death is imminent.

In "dumb" rabies, paralysis is swift; the dog seeks dark, sheltered places and is abnormally quiet. Paralysis starts with the jaws, spreads down the body, and death is quick. Contact by humans or other animals with the drool from either of these types of rabies on open skin can produce the fatal disease, so extreme haste and proper diagnosis is essential. In other words, you do not have to be bitten by a rabid dog to have the virus enter

Seven-week-old puppy owned by Beaux-Art.

Cathi Schneider enjoys a quiet moment with one of her Glimmer Glen dogs.

puppies are not protected with the colostrum normally supplied to them through the mother's milk. Puppies weaned at six to seven weeks should also be inoculated repeatedly because they will no longer be receiving mother's milk. While not all will receive protection from the serum at this early age, it should be given and they should be vaccinated once again at both nine and 12 weeks of age.

Leptospirosis vaccination should be given at four months of age with thought given to booster shots if the disease is known in the area, or in the case of show dogs which are exposed on a regular basis to many dogs from far and wide. While animal boosters are in order for distemper and hepatitis, every two or three years is sufficient for leptospirosis, unless there is an outbreak in your immediate area. The one exception should be the pregnant bitch, since there is reason to believe that inoculation might cause damage to the fetus.

Strict observance of such a vaccination schedule will not only keep your dog free of these debilitating diseases, but will prevent an epidemic in your kennel, in your locality, or to the dogs that are competing at the shows.

SNAKEBITE

As field trials, hunts, and the like become more and more popular with dog enthusiasts, the incident of snakebite becomes more of a likelihood. Dogs that are kept outdoors in runs or dogs that work the fields and roam on large estates are also likely victims.

Most veterinarians carry snakebit serum, and snakebite kits are sold to dog owners for just such a purpose. Catching a snakebite in time may mean the difference between life and death, and whether your area is populated with snakes or not, it behooves you to know what to do in case it happens to you or your dog.

Your primary concern should be to get to a doctor or veterinarian immediately. The victim should be kept as quiet as possible (excitement or activity spreads the venom through the body more quickly) and, if possible, the wound should be bled enough to clean it out before applying a tourniquet if the bite is severe.

First of all, it must be determined if the bite is from a poisonous or non-poisonous snake. If the bite carries two horseshoe-shaped pinpoints of a double row of teeth, the bite

ZL's Frito Bandito of Texas relaxes in a tree in Alvin, TX.

can be assumed to be non-poisonous. If the bite leaves two punctures or holes—the result of the two fangs carrying venom—the bite is very definitely poisonous and time is of the essence.

Recently, physicians have come up with an added help in the case of snakebite. A first aid treatment referred to as "hypothermia," which is the application of ice to the wound which lowers body temperature to a point where the venom spreads less quickly, minimizes swelling, helps prevent infection, and has some influence on numbing the pain. If ice is not readily available, the bite may be soaked in ice-cold water. But even more urgent is the need to get the victim to a hospital or a veterinarian for additional treatment.

EMERGENCIES

No matter how well you run your kennel or keep an eye on an individual dog, there will almost invariably be some emergency at some time that will require quick treatment until you get the animal to the veterinarian. The first and most important thing to remember is to keep calm! You will think more clearly and your animal will need to know he can depend on you to take care of him. However, he will be frightened and you must beware of fear biting.

Therefore, do not shower him with kisses and endearments at this time, no matter how sympathetic you feel. Comfort him reassuringly, but keep your wits about you. Before getting him to the veterinarian, try to alleviate the pain and the shock.

If you can take even a minor step in this direction it will be a help toward the final cure. Listed here are a few of the emergencies that might occur and what you can do *after* you have called the vet and told him you are coming.

BURNS

If you have been so foolish as to not turn your pot handles toward the back of the stove—for your children's sake as well as your dog's—and the dog is burned by the contents of a pot that has been knocked off its burner, apply ice or ice-cold water and treat for shock. Electrical or chemical burns are treated the same, but with an acid or alkali burn, use, respectively, a bicarbonate of soda or a vinegar solution. Check the advisability of covering the burn when you call the veterinarian.

DROWNING

Most animals love the water but sometimes get in "over their heads." Should your dog take in too much water, hold him upside

A Ben Ching Shar-Pei with a stuffed buddy.

down and open his mouth so that water can empty from the lungs, then apply artificial respiration or mouth-to-mouth resuscitation. With a large dog, hang the head over a step or off the end of a table while you hoist the rear end in the air by the back feet. Then treat for shock by covering him with a blanket.

FITS AND CONVULSIONS
Prevent the dog from thrashing about and injuring himself, cover with a blanket, and hold down until you can get him to the veterinarian.

FROSTBITE
There is no excuse for an animal getting frostbite if you are "on your toes" and

care for the animal; however, should frostbite set in, thaw out the affected area slowly by massaging with a circular motion and stimulation. Use petroleum jelly to help keep the skin from peeling off and/or drying out.

HEART ATTACK

Be sure the animal keeps breathing by applying artificial respiration. A mild stimulant may be used, and give him plenty of air. Treat for shock as well, and get him to the veterinarian quickly.

SHOCK

Shock is a state of circulatory collapse that can be induced by a severe accident, loss of blood, heart failure, or any injury to the nervous system. Until you can get the dog to the veterinarian, keep him warm by covering him with a blanket. Try to keep the dog quiet until the appropriate medication can be prescribed. Relapse is not uncommon, so the dog must be observed carefully for several days after initial shock.

SUFFOCATION

Administer artificial respiration and treat for shock with plenty of air.

SUN STROKE

Cooling the dog off immediately is essential. Ice packs, submersion in ice water, and plenty of cool air are needed.

WOUNDS

Open wounds or cuts that produce bleeding must be treated with hydrogen peroxide, and tourniquets

Ch. ZL's Onley One Son as a puppy at Shoestring Acres.

should be used if bleeding is excessive. Shock treatment must also be given, and the animal must be kept warm.

THE FIRST AID KIT

It would be sheer folly to try to operate a kennel or to keep a dog without providing for certain emergencies that are bound to crop up when there are active dogs around. Just as you would provide a first aid kit for people, you should also provide a first aid kit for the animals on the premises. The first aid kit should contain the following items:

- medicated powder
- petroleum jelly
- cotton swabs
- 1″ gauze bandage
- adhesive tape
- band-aids
- cotton gauze or balls
- boric acid powder

A trip to your veterinarian is always safest, but there are certain preliminaries for cuts and bruises of a minor nature that you can care for yourself.

Cuts, for instance, should be washed out and medicated powder or petroleum jelly applied with a bandage. The lighter the bandage the better so that the most air possible can reach the wound. Cotton swabs can be used for removing debris from the eyes, after which a mild solution of boric acid wash

Glimmer Glen's Whitney Houston at eight weeks of age. Bred and owned by Cathi Schneider.

can be applied. As for sores, use dry powder on wet sores, and petroleum jelly on dry sores. Use cotton for washing out and drying wounds.

A particular caution must be given here on bandaging. Make sure that the bandage is not too tight so as to hamper the dog's circulation. Also, make sure the bandage is applied correctly so that the dog does not bite at it trying to remove it. A great deal of damage can be done to a wound by a dog tearing at a bandage to get it off. If you

notice the dog is starting to bite at it, do it over or put something on the bandage that smells and tastes bad to him. Make sure, however, that the solution does not soak through the bandage and enter the wound. Sometimes, if it is a leg wound, a sock or stocking slipped on the dog's leg will cover the bandage edges and will also keep it clean.

HOW NOT TO POISON YOUR DOG

Ever since the appearance of Rachel Carson's book *Silent Spring*, people have been asking, "Just how dangerous are chemicals?" In the animal fancy where disinfectants, room deodorants, parasitic sprays, solutions, and aerosols are so widely used, the question has taken on even more meaning. Veterinarians are beginning to ask, "What kind of disinfectant do you use?" "Have you any fruit trees that have been sprayed recently?" When animals are brought in to their offices in a toxic condition, or for unexplained death, or when entire litters of puppies die mysteriously, there is good reason to ask such questions.

The popular practice of protecting animals against parasites has given way to their being exposed to an alarming number of commercial products, some of which are dangerous to their very lives. Even flea collars can be dangerous, especially if they get wet or somehow touch the genital regions or eyes. While some products are much more poisonous than others, great care must be taken that they be applied in proportion to the size of the dog and the area to be covered. Many a dog has been taken to the vet with an unusual skin problem that was a direct result of having been bathed with a detergent rather than a proper shampoo. Certain products that are safe for dogs can be fatal for cats. Extreme care must be taken to read all ingredients and instructions carefully before using the products on any animal.

The same caution must be given to outdoor chemicals. Dog owners must question the use of fertilizers on their lawns. Lime, for instance, can be harmful to a dog's feet. The unleashed dog that covers the neighborhood on his daily rounds is open to all sorts of tree and lawn sprays and insecticides that may prove harmful to him, if not as a poison, then as a producer of an allergy.

There are numerous products found around the house that can be lethal, such as rat poison, boric acid, hand soap, detergents, car anti-freeze, and insecticides. These are all available in the house or garage and can be tipped over easily and consumed. Many puppy fatalities are reported as a result of puppies eating mothballs. All poisons should be placed on high shelves out of the reach of *both* children and animals.

Perhaps the most readily available of all household poisons are plants. Household plants are almost all poisonous, even if taken in small quantities. Some of the most dangerous are the elephant ear, the narcissus bulb, any kind of ivy leaves, burning bush leaves, the jimson weed, the dumb cane weed, mock orange fruit, castor beans, Scottish broom seeds, the root or seed of the plant called "four o'clock," cyclamen, pimpernel, lily of the valley, the stem of the sweet pea, rhododendrons of any kind, spider lily bulbs, bayonet root, foxglove leaves, tulip bulbs, monkshood roots, azalea, wisteria, poinsettia leaves, mistletoe, hemlock, locoweed, and arrowglove. In all, there are over 500 poisonous plants in the United States. Peach, elderberry, and cherry trees can cause cyanide poisoning if the bark is consumed. Rhubarb leaves, either raw or cooked, can cause death or violent convulsions.

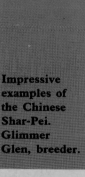

Impressive examples of the Chinese Shar-Pei. Glimmer Glen, breeder.

Glimmer Glen's Decadence Doll, owned by Sarah Schneider.

Check out your closets, fields, and grounds around your home, and especially the dog runs, to see what should be eliminated to remove the danger to your dogs.

Be on the lookout for vomiting, hard or labored breathing, whimpering, stomach cramps, and trembling as a prelude to convulsions. Any delay in a visit to your veterinarian can mean death. Take along the bottle, package, or a sample of the plant you suspect to be the cause to help the veterinarian determine the correct antidote.

The most common type of poisoning, which accounts for nearly one-fourth of all animal victims, is staphylococci–infected food. Salmonella ranks third. These can be avoided by serving fresh food and not letting it lie around in hot weather.

There are also many insect poisonings caused by animals eating cockroaches, spiders, flies, butterflies, etc. Toads and some frogs give off a fluid that can make a dog foam at the mouth—and even kill him—if he bites just a little too hard!

Some misguided dog owners think it is "cute" to let their dogs enjoy a cocktail with them before dinner. There can be serious effects resulting from encouraging a dog to drink—sneezing fits, injuries as a result of intoxication, and heart stoppage are just a few. Whiskey for medicinal purposes or beer for brood bitches should be administered only on the advice of your veterinarian.

There have been cases of severe damage and death when dogs have emptied ash trays and eaten cigarettes, resulting in nicotine poisoning. Leaving a dog alone all day in a house where there are cigarettes available on a coffee table is asking for trouble. Needless to say, the same applies to marijuana. All the ghastly side effects are as possible for the dog as for the addict, and for a person to submit an animal to this indignity is indeed despicable. Don't think it doesn't happen. Unfortunately, in all our major cities the practice is becoming more and more a problem for the veterinarian.

Be on the alert and remember that in the case of any type of poisoning, the best treatment is prevention.

ALLERGIES IN DOGS

It used to be that you recognized an allergy in your dog when he scratched out his coat and developed a large patch of raw skin or sneezed himself almost to death on certain occasions. A trip to the veterinarian involved endless discussion as to why it might be and an almost equally endless "hit and miss" cure of various salves and lotions with the hope that one of them would work. Many times the condition would correct itself before a definite cure was affected.

However, during the 1970s through preliminary findings at the University of Pennsylvania Veterinary School there evolved a diagnosis for allergies that eliminated the need for skin sensitivity tests. It is called RAST, and is a radioallergosobant test performed with a blood serum sample. It is not even necessary in all cases for the veterinarian to see the dog.

A cellulose disc laced with a suspected allergen, is placed in the serum, and if the dog is allergic to that particular allergen the serum will contain a specific antibody that adheres to the allergen on the disc. The disc is placed in a radioactively "labeled" antiserum that is attracted to that particular antibody. The antiserum binds with the antibody and can be detected with a radiation

Shoestring Acres puppies getting into mischief in their own back yard.

counter.

Furthermore, the scientists at the University of Pennsylvania also found that the RAST test has shown to be a more accurate diagnostic tool than skin testing because it measures the degree, and not merely the presence, of allergic reactions.

DO ALL DOGS CHEW?

The answer to the question about whether all dogs chew is an emphatic *yes,* and the answer is even more emphatic in the case of puppies.

Chewing is the best possible method of cutting teeth and exercising gums. Every puppy goes through this teething process, yet it can be destructive if the puppy uses shoes or table corners or rugs instead of the proper item for the best possible results. All dogs should have a Nylabone available for chewing, not only to teethe on but also for inducing growth of the permanent teeth, to assure normal jaw development, and to settle the permanent teeth solidly in the jaws. Chewing on a Nylabone also has a cleaning effect and serves as a "massage" for the gums, keeping down the formation of the tartar that erodes tooth enamel.

When you see a puppy pick up an object to chew, immediately remove it from his mouth with a sharp "No!" and replace the object with a Nylabone. Puppies take anything and everything into their mouths so they should be provided with several Nylabones to prevent damage to the household. This same Nylabone eliminates the need for the kind of "bone" which may chip your dog's mouth, stomach, or intestinal walls. Cooked bones, soft enough to be powdered and added to the food, are also permissible if you have the patience to prepare them, but Nylabone serves all the purposes of bones for chewing that your dog may require, so why take a chance on meat bones?

Electrical cords and wires of any kind present a special danger that must be eliminated during puppyhood, and glass dishes that can be broken and played with are also hazardous.

Chewing can also be a sign of frustration or nervousness. Dogs sometimes chew for spite, if owners leave them alone too long or too often. Bitches will sometimes chew if their puppies are taken away from them too soon; insecure puppies often chew, thinking that they're nursing. Puppies that chew wool, blankets, carpet corners, or certain other types of materials may have a nutritional deficiency or something lacking in their diet. Sometimes a

puppy will crave the starch that might be left in material after washing. Perhaps the articles have been near something that tastes good and have retained the odor of food.

The act of chewing has no connection with particular breeds or ages, any more than there is a logical reason for dogs to dig holes outdoors or dig on wooden floors indoors.

So we repeat, it is up to you to be on guard at all times until the need—or habit—passes.

HIP DYSPLASIA

Hip dysplasia, or HD, is one of the most widely discussed of all animal afflictions, since it has appeared in varying degrees in just about every breed of dog. True, the larger breeds seem most susceptible, but it has hit the small breeds and is beginning to be

Ch. Temple Toi Temptations reveals the proper brush coat length as well as the red color which calls for light pigmentation.

recognized in cats as well.

While HD in man has been recorded as far back as 370 BC, HD in dogs was more than likely referred to as rheumatism until veterinary research came into the picture. In 1935 Dr. Otto Schales, at Angell Memorial Hospital in Boston, wrote a paper on hip dysplasia and classified the four degrees of dysplasia of the hip joints as follows:

- Grade 1—slight (poor fit between ball socket)
- Grade 2—moderate (moderate but obvious shallowness of the socket)
- Grade 3—severe (socket quite flat)
- Grade 4—very severe (complete displacement of head of femur at early age)

HD is an incurable, hereditary, though not necessarily congenital, disease of the hip sockets. It is transmitted as a dominant trait with irregular manifestations. Puppies appear normal at birth but the constant wearing away of the socket means the animal moves more and more on muscle, thereby presenting a lameness, a difficulty in getting up, and pain in advanced cases.

The degree of severity can be determined around six months of age, but its presence can be noticed from two months of age. The problem is determined by X-ray, and if pain is present it can be relieved temporarily by medication. Exercise should be avoided

Doll's Litzi of Albright, owned by Carl and Harry Bence and bred by Doll Weil.

Bruce Lee's Kilo Tu Yang, owned by Vivien Kelly, Ben Ching Kennels.

since motion encourages the wearing away of the bone surfaces.

Dogs with HD should not be shown or bred, if quality in the breed is to be maintained. It is essential to check a pedigree for dogs known to be dysplastic before breeding, since this disease can be dormant for many generations.

The same condition can also affect the elbow joints and is known as elbow dysplasia. This also causes lameness, and dogs so affected should not be used for breeding.

THE UNITED STATES REGISTRY

In the United States we have a central Hip Dysplasia Foundation, known as the OFA (Orthopedic Foundation for Animals). This HD control registry was formed in 1966. X-rays are sent for expert evaluation by qualified radiologists.

All you need do for complete information on getting an X-ray for your dog is to write to the Orthopedic Foundation for Animals at 817 Virginia Ave., Columbia, MO 65201, and request their dysplasia packet. There is no charge for this kit. It contains an envelope large enough to hold your X-ray film (which you will have taken by your own veterinarian), and a drawing showing how to position the dog properly for X-rays. There is also an application card for proper identification of the dog. Then, hopefully, your dog will be certified "normal." You will be given a registry number which you can put on his pedigree, use in your advertising, and rest assured that your breeding program is in good order.

All X-rays should be sent to the address above. Any other information you might wish to have may be requested from Mrs. Robert Bower, OFA, Route 1, Constantine, MO 49042.

We cannot urge strongly enough the importance of doing this. While it involves time and effort, the reward in the long run will more than pay for your trouble. To see the heartbreak of parents and children when their beloved dog has to be put to sleep because of severe hip dysplasia as the result of bad breeding is a sad experience. Don't let this happen to you or to those who will purchase your puppies!

Additionally, we should mention that there is a method of palpation to determine the extent of affliction. This can be painful if the animal is not properly prepared for the examination. There have also been attempts to replace the animal's femur and socket. This is not only expensive, but the percentage of success is small.

For those who refuse to put their dog down, there is a new surgical technique that can relieve pain but in no way constitutes a cure. This technique involves the severing of the pectinius muscle which, for some unknown reason, brings relief from pain over a period of many months— even up to two years. Two veterinary colleges in the United States are performing this operation at the present time. However, the owner must also give permission to "de-sex" the dogs at the time of the muscle severance. This is a safety measure to help stamp out hip dysplasia, since obviously the condition itself remains and can be passed on through generations.

The British Veterinary Association (BVA) has made an attempt to control the spread of HD by appointing a panel of members of their profession, who have made a special study of the disease, to read X-rays.

Dogs over one year of age may be X-rayed and certified as free. Forms are completed in triplicate to verify the tests. One copy remains with the panel, one copy is for the owner's veterinarian, and one for the owner. A record is also sent to the British Kennel Club for those wishing to check on a particular dog for breeding purposes.

GERIATRICS

If you originally purchased good healthy stock and cared for your dog throughout his life, there is no reason why you cannot expect your dog to live to a ripe old age. With research and the remarkable foods produced for dogs, especially in this past decade, his chances of longevity have increased considerably. If you have cared for him well, your dog will be a sheer delight in his old age, just as he was while in his prime.

We can assume you have fed him properly if he is not too fat. Have you ever noticed how fat people usually have fat dogs because they indulge their dog's appetite as they do their own? If there has been no great illness, then you will find that very little additional care and attention are needed to keep him well. Exercise is still essential, as are proper food, booster shots, and tender loving care.

Even if a heart condition develops, there is still no reason to believe your dog cannot live to an old age. A diet may be necessary, along with medication and limited exercise, to keep the condition under control. In the case of deafness or partial blindness, additional care must be taken to protect the dog, but neither infirmity will in any way shorten his life. Prolonged exposure to temperature variances; overeating; excessive exercise; lack of sleep; or being housed with

Beaux-Art Chocolate Elite at eight weeks of age demonstrates the proud carriage of the Shar-Pei.

younger, more active dogs may take an unnecessary toll on the dog's energies and induce serious trouble. Good judgment, periodic veterinary checkups, and individual attention will keep your dog with you for many added years.

When discussing geriatrics, the question of when a dog becomes old or aged is usually asked. We have all heard the old saying that one year of a dog's life is equal to seven years in a human. This theory is strictly a matter of opinion, and must remain so, since so many outside factors enter into how quickly each individual dog "ages." Recently, a new chart was devised that is more realistically equivalent:

DOG	MAN
6 months	10 years
1 year	15 years
2 years	24 years
3 years	28 years
4 years	32 years
5 years	36 years
6 years	40 years
7 years	44 years
8 years	48 years
9 years	52 years
10 year	56 years
15 years	76 years
21 years	100 years

It must be remembered that such things as serious illnesses, poor food and housing, general neglect, and poor beginnings as puppies will take their toll of a dog's general health and age him more quickly than a dog that has led a normal, healthy life. Let your veterinarian help you determine an age bracket for your dog in his later years.

While good care should prolong your dog's life, there are several "old age" disorders to watch for no matter how well he may be doing. The tendency toward obesity is the most common, but constipation is another. Aging teeth and a slowing down of the digestive processes may hinder digestion and cause constipation, just as any major change in diet can bring on diarrhea. There is also the possibility of loss or impairment of hearing or eyesight which will also tend to make the dog wary and distrustful. Other behavioral changes may result as well, such as crankiness, loss of patience, and lack of interest; these are the most obvious changes. Other ailments may manifest themselves in the form of rheumatism, arthritis, tumors and warts, heart disease, kidney infections, male prostatism, and female disorders. Of course, all these require a veterinarian's checking the degree of seriousness and proper treatment.

THE CURSE OF ALLERGY

The heartbreak of a child being forced to give up a beloved pet because he is suddenly found to be allergic to it is a sad but true story. Many families claim to be unable to have dogs at all; others seem to be able only to enjoy them on a restricted basis. Many children know animals only through occasional visits to a friend's house or the zoo.

While modern veterinary science has produced some brilliant allergists, the field is still working on a solution for those who suffer from exposure to their pets. There is no permanent cure as yet.

Over the last quarter of a century there have been many attempts at a permanent cure, but none have proven successful because the treatment was needed too frequently, or was too expensive to maintain over extended periods of time.

However, we find that most people who are allergic to their animals are also allergic to a variety of other things as well. By eliminating the other irritants, and by taking

Nap time at Beaux-Art, Golden Nugget and Peaches settle in.

medication given for the control of allergies in general, many are able to keep pets on a restricted basis. This may necessitate the dog's living outside the house, being groomed at a professional grooming parlor instead of by the owner, or merely being kept out of the bedroom at night. A discussion of this "balance" factor with your medical and veterinary doctors may give new hope to those willing to try.

A paper presented by Mathilde M. Gould, MD, a New York allergist, before the American Academy of Allergists in the 1960s and reported in the September-October 1964 issue of the *National Humane Review*

magazine, offered new hope to those who are allergic by a method referred to as hyposensitization. You may wish to write to the magazine and request the article for discussion of your individual problem with your medical doctors.

Surely, since the sixties there have been additional advances in the field of allergy since so many people—and animals—are affected in so many ways.

DOG INSURANCE

Much has been said for and against canine insurance, and much more will be said before this kind of protection for a dog becomes universal and/or practical. There has been

Doll's Tish-Chu of Albright, owned by Pam Hains and bred by Doll Weil of Doll Acre Farms.

Three-month-old future Ch. Glimmer Glen's Chit-E-Chit-E Bang Bang. Bred by Cathi Schneider and owned by Doll Weil.

talk of establishing a Blue Cross-type plan similar to the one now existing for humans. However, the best insurance for your dog is *you!* Nothing compensates for tender loving care. Like the insurance policies for humans, there will be a lot of fine print in the contracts revealing that the dog is not covered after all. These limited conditions usually make the acquisition of dog insurance expensive and virtually worthless.

Blanket coverage policies for kennels or establishments that board or groom dogs can be an advantage, especially in transporting dogs to and from their premises. For the one-dog owner, however, whose dog is a constant companion, the cost for limited coverage is not necessary.

Five-month-old Oriental Treasures Pebbles, owned by Ben Ching Kennels.

Perhaps you are fortunate enough to have a relative, child, spouse, or friend who would take over immediately, if only on a temporary basis. Perhaps you have already left instructions in your last will and testament for your pet's housing, as well as a stipend for its care.

Provide definite instructions before a disaster occurs and your dogs are carted off to the pound to be destroyed, or stolen by commercially inclined neighbors with "resale" in mind. It is a simple thing to instruct your lawyer about your wishes in the event of sickness or death. Leave instructions as to feeding, etc., posted on your kennel room or kitchen bulletin board, or wherever your kennel records are kept. Also, tell several people what you are doing and why. If you prefer to keep such instructions private, merely place them in sealed envelopes in a known place with directions that they are to be opened only in the event of your death. Eliminate the danger of your animals suffering in the event of an emergency that prevents your personal care of them.

THE HIGH COST OF BURIAL

Pet cemeteries are mushrooming across the nation. Here, as with humans, the sky can be the limit for those who wish to bury their pets ceremoniously. The costs of plots and satin-lined caskets, grave stones, flowers, etc., run the gamut to match the emotions and means of the owner.

IN THE EVENT OF YOUR DEATH

This is a morbid thought perhaps, but ask yourself the question, "If death were to strike at this moment, what would become of my dogs?"

KEEPING RECORDS

Whether you have one dog or a kennel full of them, it is wise to keep written records. It takes only a few moments to record dates of inoculations, trips to the vet, tests for worms, etc. It can avoid confusion or mistakes or having your dog not covered with immunization if too much time elapses between shots because you have to guess at the date of the last shot.

Make the effort to keep all dates in writing rather than trying to commit them to memory. A rabies injection date can be a problem if you have to recall that "Fido had the shot the day Aunt Mary got back from her trip abroad, and, let's see, I guess that was around the end of June."

In an emergency, these records may prove their value if your veterinarian cannot be reached and you have to call on another, or if you move and have no case history on your dog for the new veterinarian. In emergencies, one does not always think clearly or accurately, and if dates, types of serums used, and other information are a matter of record, the veterinarian can act more quickly and with more confidence.

A Ta Yang daughter, bred and owned by Ben Ching Kennels.

A PRAYER FOR ANIMALS

Hear our humble prayer, O God, for our friends the animals, especially for animals who are suffering; for any that are hunted or lost or deserted or frightened or hungry; for all that must be put to death. We entreat for them all Thy mercy and pity, and for those who deal with them we ask a heart of compassion and gentle hands and kindly words. Make us, ourselves, to be true friends to animals and so to share the blessings of the merciful.

Albert Schweitzer

Dim Sum of Tai-Ko, owned by Jeanne Wood of Los Angelos, CA.

— Index —

For the sake of convenience, all titles have been removed from dogs' names. Page numbers in *italic* refer to illustrations.

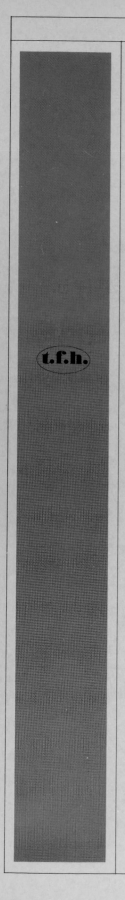

The Book of the Shar-Pei
TS-150